MASTERS' SECRETS

of

DEER
HUNTING

by John E. Phillips

**Book I in the Deer Hunting Library
by Larsen's Outdoor Publishing**

ISBN 0-936513-14-7

Library of Congress 91-090327

Published by:

LARSEN'S OUTDOOR PUBLISHING
2640 Elizabeth Place
Lakeland, FL 33813

PRINTED IN THE UNITED STATES OF AMERICA

6 7 8 9 10

DEDICATION

To the men who made this book possible, Don Taylor, Dr. Robert Sheppard, Bob Zaiglin, Dr. Keith Causey, Ronnie Groom, Dr. Larry Marchinton and Dr. Karl Miller. They're all good friends and willing teachers, as well as master deer hunters.

ACKNOWLEDGEMENTS

No author writes a book alone. Many hands must pull together to complete a manuscript. I want to thank my wife, Denise Phillips, for her editing, and Marjolyn McLellan, Mary Ann Armstrong and Cara Dee Clark for their help. For their production of the book and taking care of all the little details that have produced this finished product, I want to thank Lilliam and Larry Larsen.

PREFACE

A deer hunt is much like a football game. The hunter and the quarterback must know exactly which calls to make as the hunt or the game progresses. Often some extra effort and a few more inches can spell the difference in victory or defeat. When the conditions change, knowing which calls will work and which calls won't can determine the outcome of the day.

To become a great quarterback or a proficient deer hunter, both athletes must learn from the masters of their sports. Learning tried and true tactics, new plays and better offenses and defenses are the critical keys for success in every sport. Developing a strategic game plan before the hunt or the football game is essential to winning the day.

By studying the methods of hunting offered in <u>The Masters' Secrets of Deer Hunting</u>, a deer hunter should be able to save himself five to six years of in-the-woods experience. The men in this book have devoted themselves to the study of hunting whitetail deer. Let them teach you, and you'll increase your odds for bagging a buck this season.

TABLE OF CONTENTS

ABOUT THE AUTHOR

For more than three decades, John E. Phillips has hunted the whitetail deer. He even chose to attend Livingston University in deer-rich Southwest Alabama to be able to deer hunt at least four days a week from mid-October until the last day of January during his college years until graduation.

Phillips also has been a student of deer and deer hunting as a part-time taxidermist and an active outdoor writer and photographer for more than 20-years for both newspapers and magazines. Phillips, the author of eight outdoor books including: Alabama Outdoors Cookbook, How To Make More Profits In Taxidermy, Catch More Crappie, Outdoor Life's Complete Turkey Hunting, Bass Fishing With The Skeeter Pros, North American Hunting Club's Turkey Hunting Tactics, Deer & Fixings and Fish and Fixings, has had more than 1,000 articles published on hunting deer. An active member of Outdoor Writers Association of America, Southeastern Outdoors Press Association, Alabama Press Association and Outdoors Photographic League, Phillips has won numerous awards for excellence in writing magazine and newspaper articles and outdoor books.

Phillips feels fortunate to have hunted with some of the greatest deer hunters of our day, which has made him passionate for the sport. He has taken deer with bow and arrow, blackpowder rifles, shotguns and conventional rifles. He has hunted the mountains, plains, swamps, forests and croplands of the U.S. Phillips has learned the art of deer hunting from some of the best hunters in the nation and has brought this knowledge to you in The Masters' Secrets of Deer Hunting.

CHAPTER 1

HOW TO BE A SUCCESSFUL DEER HUNTER
With Don Taylor

WHAT ARE THE REQUIREMENTS for successful deer hunting? Many of us will seek the answer to this question each season by learning how to find a buck, how to take that buck, what the latest hunting techniques are, what super duper lure can be used to bring bucks in - even when they don't want to come in - and where that secret, hidden pocket is that no one knows about where a hunter can be 99 percent sure of taking a deer.

Having Self-Discipline
The hunter must be able to control himself and to self-discipline his actions. Knowing what can be done does not necessarily mean a hunter does what needs to be done.

I've met many hunters who understand that to take a trophy buck they'll have to sit in one place all day and wait for that buck to show up. But they can't force themselves to stay in one spot for the time required. These outdoorsmen know what to do intellectually, but they can't discipline their bodies to do what they need to do.

Stalk hunting for deer is another prime example of a hunter's self-discipline. Most stalk hunters believe the adage, "The slower a stalker goes, the more game he sees." So they deliberately walk slowly. However, they see a bend in the road and say to themselves, "I bet if I hurry up, get to that bend and look around it, a deer will be standing just on the other side."

Once they slip up to the bend in the road and peep around the bend, they don't see any deer. They may keep watching around that bend for all of two minutes or until they convince themselves no deer are present in the

13

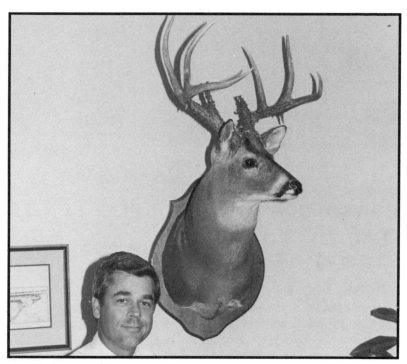

Don Taylor has been hunting whitetail deer most of his life. A student of the sport, he bags trophy-sized animals each season. Taylor and his hunting tactics have been the subject of several national and regional magazine articles, and he also has been featured in numerous newspaper columns.

area. Then they reason, "Since I can't see a deer for at least 50 yards, I mustn't waste my time staying here. I'll go on down the road about 50 yards, stop and look."

Each time these woodsmen pause to search, they talk themselves into believing no deer is in the vicinity.

Reason dictates that if no deer is where they are looking, they need to be watching somewhere else and not wasting their time in that area. Instead of taking three to four hours to cover a half a mile while stalking, they move three to four miles in an hour and a half and wonder why they haven't spotted any game.

To be a good deer hunter, every time you take one step forward, you need to be totally convinced that a deer is standing just in front of you only if you can see it. You must take plenty of time to try and spot a deer. Every time I move one step forward, I can see from 40 to 60 percent more of the

Learning the discipline of staying put in your treestand is a key to success.

woods than I can one step back. I discipline myself to move slowly enough to spot everything I can possibly see before I take another step.

I have to constantly remind myself that I am not looking for a deer but instead am attempting to spot an ear tip, the black circle of a deer's eye, a parallel line to the ground, which will indicate a deer's back, the small tip of an ivory- colored antler or a leg protruding out from behind a tree. The little things are what give away a deer's position. To observe those small things, the hunter must discipline himself to take the time required to see all he can.

Using Proper Equipment

Although the terrain an outdoorsman hunts, and the method he uses will dictate the type of equipment he needs, certain pieces of equipment are

If you walk too quickly, you may walk past the buck you are trying to take.

essential for successful deer hunting anywhere. Being able to see what's in front of you is critical to being able to bag a buck. Always carry a pair of pocket size binoculars with you. Small, lightweight binoculars will enable you to see well enough at 100 yards to identify a deer.

I constantly use my binoculars. Many times I will see something white bouncing on a limb. My brain may say that the white blur is some kind of small bird, but as we all know, human eyes can be deceived. I use my binoculars to be sure. Most of the time, it is a bird. However, perhaps 10 percent of the time that patch of white I've seen bouncing will be the white inside of a deer's ear, an antler tip or a tail swishing. Without utilizing the binoculars, I may have walked off and left the buck.

Besides binoculars, a productive hunter must have a rifle he can shoot accurately and one he has shot accurately many times before he goes into the woods. If the hunter doesn't know where the bullet will land when he squeezes the trigger, then if a deer steps in front of him, that hunter isn't sure he can take the deer. But if you fire your rifle enough times at varying distances on a range and learn within a half inch where the bullet is going to land when you squeeze the trigger, then you probably will bag the buck.

To shoot accurately, you must have a scope you can use in your hunting situation, and you must mount your scope correctly. For woods hunting, most of the time you need a scope that is 3X or 4X strong. If you are hunting with a variable scope, for instance a 3-9 scope, then always set it at the lowest magnification to give you the widest field of view. If you are stalk or stand hunting and a deer comes in close to you with your scope set at 9X, picking the target to shoot at will be extremely difficult, because the deer is too close. But if you have your scope set on the widest field of view and the lowest magnification, when a deer walks in at 15 to 40 yards, he will make an easy target. If you do happen to spot a deer at 75 to 100 yards out, you will have plenty of time to screw your scope from 3X to 9X before you take the shot.

Besides binoculars, an accurate rifle and a well- mounted, quality scope, the successful hunter must wear clothes that are comfortable and that camouflage him.

Knowing The Woods

One mistake many new deer hunters make is running all over the country trying to kill a deer. Deer hunters are much like bass fishermen who, when they hear about a new fishing hotspot, leave their home lakes thinking they will catch more and bigger fish somewhere else. But actually, the more you know about the land you plan to hunt, the greater your odds are of not only taking a deer but bagging a trophy deer.

When I say to learn the land you hunt, I not only mean know your way around the land so you don't get lost but also to learn where the food for the deer is, where the bedding areas are, where the trails are and where the deer go when the hunting pressure is high. Each year, discover something new and different about your hunting land.

Understanding Deer Movement

Do you know where the most deer are taken on the property you hunt? Where are most of the deer seen? Where do the deer scrape year after year? About what week do the deer rut, each year? What is the deer's preferred food source each week of the season? Where is that food source located on your property? Where on the land you hunt will no one ever think to look for a deer? How do deer movement patterns change from...

    ... before bow season to during bow season,

    ... at the beginning of gun season,

    ... during the middle of gun season,

    ... while the rut is going on and

    ... at the end of deer season?

All the answers to these questions will help you to think like a trophy deer. Once you begin to learn the deer's movement, behavior, feeding, and mating patterns, then you will come closer to being a successful deer hunter. Compiling this much information requires a conscious effort on a hunter's part to keep records and to notice what he is observing in the woods every time he is hunting. To learn how to hunt deer, you must study deer, just like you do any other subject.

Often hunters stumble through the woods relying on information they've heard from someone else rather than doing their own research. Remember that if the man who is giving you the information knows how to take the deer, he already will have bagged the bucks. I feel a hunter must rely on his own research and study to understand more about the deer he hunts.

Having Confidence Hunting New Regions

A dedicated deer hunter always must assume he can hunt regions no one else thinks can be hunted. Deer know where hunters won't go. At least, big, smart, trophy bucks do and that's where they hide during the season. Thick patches of cane, huge briar thickets and head-high clearcuts where visibility may be only six feet or less will be passed up by most hunters.

No matter how dense the cover, there is either a trail, a drainage ditch, a creek or an open spot somewhere in that cover. Many times I have gone into areas that have head-high growth for 30 yards when all of a sudden I'll come into a clearing where I can see for 30 to 40 yards. Or else I may find a drainage ditch or some type of break in the cover that permits me a clear view for 10 to 20 yards. If I get into that thick cover and can't discover a place to see from, then I'll cut a shooting lane- or perhaps two or three - each 20 to 30 yards in length. But I never cut a trail into heavy cover, because then another hunter may use that same trail to move in to where I'm hunting.

To consistently bag deer, you must know exactly where the bullet will land when you squeeze the trigger.

Anytime you hear hunters say, "You can't hunt this region or that area, it's too thick," then you know that's exactly the spot where you must hunt if you are going to take a buck. The more hunting pressure exerted on a place, the thicker cover you will have to hunt to harvest a nice buck. Many times the difference in success or failure is how well you learn to hunt places where other sportsmen think deer cannot be hunted.

Don Taylor is shown with the two big bucks he bagged in less than a week in an area no one else would hunt.

Having Confidence About Bagging Bucks

The most successful deer hunters have faith they will bag bucks. Some outdoorsmen are defeated too easily. They have carefully researched to understand where a deer probably will be, they know their rifles shoot accurately enough to take deer, and they can see deer with either their naked eyes or their binoculars. However, they still may be defeated if they hunt an area five or six times and a buck doesn't show up. But if all my research says a deer should be at a certain place, I'll continue to go to that spot, even if bagging that deer takes several years.

I had one such place on a piece of property I hunted. The area met all of the requirements of thick, almost impenetrable, cover and was a natural hideout for bucks when hunting pressure was the greatest. Also this region was full of deer signs, including scrapes and rubs, and no one else hunted this region but me.

I spotted a big buck in this area but never did get a shot at him. I hunted that place for two years before I ever took a deer. But not only did I bag a trophy buck out of that region the third year I hunted it, I harvested two trophy bucks within a week of each other out of that one sanctuary.

Learning Something New On Every Hunt

I realize I don't understand everything about deer hunting. But I try to learn something every time I go into the woods. I'm constantly thinking about where a deer should be and what he should be doing. I'm adding vital research each season that will help me become a better deer hunter. I'm happy to pass on the information I've learned to help others enjoy the sport of deer hunting I love so much.

CHAPTER 2

DETECTING DEER MOVEMENT
THROUGH SCOUTING
With Dr. Robert Sheppard

TWO METHODS OF HUNTING will bag a buck. One is luck, which is a factor that a majority of hunters in many areas depend on, and the other requires experience - knowing the deer, his movement and behavior patterns.

Being able to predict deer movement is the stock in trade of the hunter who bags a buck year after year. Very little guess work is involved in this type of hunting. The sportsman takes a set of given facts, studies the terrain, the available food, the deer's mating habits and the weather, correlates them with deer signs he finds in his area and comes up with a hunt plan that logically should put him in a position to see, and hopefully bag, a deer.

Actually the hunter's mind is the ultimate weapon. Like an onboard computer, an outdoorsman feeds in data, the information is processed between his ears, and the answer of where the buck should show up on any given day is fed out and put into the outgoing box of his intellect. Let's look at the factors that are fed into a knowledgeable hunter's brain and see how he comes up with hunt plans that consistently pay off in buck sightings.

Understanding Deer

To be consistently successful, a deer hunter must adopt a philosophy which dictates that scouting is far more important and critical to hunter success than shooting. The effective hunter will spend 80-percent of his time in the woods scouting and trying to determine where and when a deer

Dr. Robert Sheppard has taught schools about bowhunting for deer, hunting with blackpowder for deer and rifle hunting for deer and hunts them more than 40 days per year. Because of Sheppard's medical training, he studies the sport of deer hunting with a researcher's eye and often notices details overlooked by most deer hunters. This can make the difference in a successful and an unsuccessful hunt.

Scout before the season to find a buck like this.

should show up and only 20 percent of his time in an attempt to take a deer.

Less knowledgeable hunters will spend 80 percent of their time wandering around in the woods or sitting on a treestand because they find a few deer tracks or some droppings. Then these same men only will spend 20 percent of their time trying to predict where the deer will show up.

But as a hunter once told me, "The most important deer tracks to the hunter are the ones the deer is standing in when the hunter is ready to shoot."

In most areas of the country, you will find several consistent hunters who seem to always bag their bucks within the first two hours of the opening day of deer season. Although luck plays a role in their success, if you question them closely, you will find out that before the season opens they have spent days and weeks studying their deer, picking their stand sites and paying close attention to the details that result in their taking bucks.

But there are no short cuts. To regularly take deer year after year, you have to spend more time scouting than you do trying to shoot a deer. Three times of the year are the most productive for scouting - before the season, during the season and at the end of the season.

Scouting Before The Season

The deer's movement patterns before the season starts are the same ones he will follow naturally and normally when he is not spooked and has no hunting pressure exerted on him. This type of scouting is primarily for the bowhunter, the blackpowder shooter and may hold true for the first one or two days of gun season. But when the woods are full of hunters and deer are moving more from fright than for any other reason, these patterns often do not work.

I begin to scout four to six weeks before deer season starts. If you start any sooner than that, the deer's feeding patterns may change, and the food they have depended on during the summer may not be the same food they are relying on during the season. If you don't know what foods the deer are feeding on or probably will be feeding on during this four to six week period prior to the beginning of deer season, check with other hunters or the state conservation officer in your hunting area.

Primarily early season scouting is for deer moving toward or away from their feeding areas. In many regions of the country, one of the best places to find deer is around agricultural crops. For instance, let's say a cornfield is bordered by a woodlot. The easiest method for patterning deer in a cornfield is to walk the edge of the field and look for tracks. But just locating tracks on the edge of a cornfield is not enough evidence to justify setting up a treestand or taking a stand close to that set of tracks going into the field.

To increase your chances of taking a deer, you need to pinpoint where tracks go into the field and come out of the field at the same point, which is where the likelihood of catching a deer entering or leaving a field is the greatest. Deer generally will come through the same region day in and day out, but they also will meander through an area. If they start from a different point to move into the field on a particular day, they may use the same point to go out from the field. Or if they come into the field from the place you've predetermined, then they may meander out in another

Scouting the edges of a cornfield will tell you where to look for a buck.

direction. But usually, deer will prefer to use one or two places along the edge of a field for entering a field. Most often the deer will want to enter a field from either corners of the field that back into the woods or from the area that seems to funnel back into the woods.

The best way to scout a field is immediately after rain. The tracks will be fresh, and you can pick the places with the most deer movement that reveal tracks going in both directions. This tactic will work during the first few weeks of bow season usually -depending on hunting pressure -because deer will pattern the same way day after day without a number of hunter encounters.

Besides a cornfield, this tactic works on any type of food source you can locate early in the season. During those first two weeks of the season, you can hunt very close to a food source.

Scouting During The Season

After deer have felt hunting pressure, their movement patterns change, which often will occur after the second week of bow season, if considerable pressure has been put on the animals from other hunters. Because the deer realize they're having hunter encounters during daylight hours, they'll begin to feed after dark and stay away from their food sources until night. Therefore treestands and ground blinds will have to be moved from the food source to another place if you want to consistently bag deer.

But to know where to move your treestand to, additional scouting is required. One of the signs that indicates a hunter should begin to scout for a new place to put his treestand is when he sees deer entering the field from several different directions. He may find that when he moves his stand to set up an ambush, the deer still won't consistently come out in the same place every day. He also may notice that he does not see as many deer move into the field during daylight hours. But after a rain, he observes just as many tracks in the field as he has at the first of the season.

To put your stand in a more productive area, the most effective technique is to back that stand up to a point in the woods the deer are coming into prior to entering the field after dark. To locate this region, I scout on the days when the weather or wind conditions are not right for hunting.

Common sense is your best tool to find that staging area after the deer have quit showing up in the field. The most reliable signs for locating deer are finding places in the woods where the deer's feet hit the ground regularly.

Go to the trail where you've hunted effectively during the early season, and follow it away from the food source into the woods. I have gotten down on my hands and knees to track deer further back into the woods away from a primary food source two to three weeks after bow season has begun.

Using this tracking method may not help you understand the total deer movement pattern. However, you will have a better picture of what the deer are doing and will know where you should place your treestand than you will have had by sitting on the edge of the field waiting for the deer to show up.

You may backtrack one deer 100 yards and find an area where two or three trails cross. Or, you may continue to follow a trail and locate the edge of a slough where 40 deer walk down that slough edge regularly. By following one deer trail away from the food source, more than likely you will find an area where many of the deer that are using that field as a food

During the season, bucks often will move and feed at night.

source will concentrate prior to entering their feeding ground. Once you discover an area like this, you will see many tracks going in both directions. That's where you want to set up your stand for the next week or two of bow season or for the first day or two of gun season.

However, instead of relying totally on one of these staging regions away from the field, the consistent hunter will follow four or five trails out of the field going in different directions which will lead him to four or five various staging areas. In each one of these staging areas, he will locate a tree for his treestand. If he is a bowhunter, he will cut shooting lanes in four directions from the tree where he plans to place his stand.

Also with his compass, he will determine what direction his treestand will be facing so he will know which way the wind must be blowing from to be able to hunt out of that stand. If his treestand faces to the North, then

29

the best time for him to hunt out of that stand to keep his scent from being carried into his hunting area will be when he has a prevailing north, northwest or northeast wind. Using this system of patterning deer, the hunter will have at least one treestand he can hunt in the deer's staging area - no matter what the wind condition is.

After the sportsman has taken his deer from one of these regions or has shot at and missed the deer in these staging areas, the deer begin to learn they are in danger when they enter these staging zones. They will start showing up in lesser numbers and finally not at all during the daylight hours. Then the deer will wait until later in the evening to enter the field or come out earlier in the morning, which makes successful deer hunting harder. When you begin to backtrack the deer even further from the staging area, the trailing becomes more difficult, because more leaves are on the ground and following the deer trails becomes more difficult.

Scouting The End Of The Season

The more you look at deer tracks and the harder you search for tracks, the better you should be able to interpret what the deer are doing when they've made the tracks. So far we've found the deer at his primary food source, which we have designated as a field. We've backtracked him through what we've called a staging area where several deer crossings meet and is where he seems to wait for the cover of darkness to enter the field.

Now we have to go even further into the woods to find the holding area where the deer stay during daylight hours when the hunting pressure is intense, which is the most difficult pattern to try and interpret. But if you can follow a deer track and find some type of thick cover - a briar thicket, a pine thicket, a cut-over field or some kind of heavy foliage where the deer have plenty of cover to hide in - then you have located a region to scout for your end-of-the-season hunting.

Scouting thickets is much like scouting at the beginning of the season. Just because you find tracks coming into a thicket or leaving a thicket doesn't mean you have enough information to set up a treestand or a ground blind to try and take a deer at that particular point. Instead, walk all the way around the edge of the thicket. Find tracks that are going both into and out of the thicket at the same place. If the thicket is large enough, and more than one deer is utilizing this cover, you may be able to find several places on the edge where the tracks go both in and out of the thicket.

Place a treestand there, or designate a tree or a ground blind site for a stand. Take your compass out, and determine which way your stand must

At the end of the season, sometimes bucks like this one will be found in thick cover.

be facing and which way you will have to approach that stand with a favorable wind. Then you can plan your hunt and decide which stand you will hunt out of according to wind direction on the morning of your hunt.

The advantage to these stands is you can catch your deer in the mornings coming from the food source and going into the thicket or in the middle of the day if they have been spooked by another hunter coming into the thicket. These late season thicket patterns may be your best, all-day hunting. All of these patterns work well during bow season and in areas during the gun season with little or no hunter pressure.

At the end of the season, strict attention must be paid to every detail. The deer are alerted and looking for danger. Although the wind is a key factor for keeping the hunter's scent out of his hunting area, equally as important is the sportsman's approach to the stand.

When gun season is on, I take a rake into the woods with me and rake a path from my treestand back 150 yards toward where I enter the woods. Then on the day I hunt I can walk to my stand without making any noise on the morning I plan to hunt. Whereas I normally take 15 minutes to get to my stand during the first part of the season, I may spend an hour covering the same distance to reach my stand in the late part of the season to keep from spooking the deer.

I also try and use permanent stands or ladder stands in the late season. Then I make little or no noise when I climb into my treestand. The most difficult deer to pattern and to hunt is a deer that has spent all season long learning what hunters do and when they do it.

By investing more time scouting and studying deer and their movement patterns and learning where they feed, where they wait to feed and where they hold when hunting pressure is on, you will be better able to predict at what point in the woods to place your treestand or ground blind for an effective ambush. If you spend more time learning about deer than you do hunting, then you will take more deer than even those who hunt the most.

CHAPTER 3

SCOUTING AFTER THE SEASON

With Don Taylor, Dr. Robert Sheppard and Bob Zaiglin

SPORTSMEN WHO CONSISTENTLY take deer each season hunt all year long by also taking the time to scout after each season. The information that hunters can learn about deer and their habits, haunts, behavior patterns and movement patterns will be invaluable for the next season. Learning about other hunters and where they hunt may often be the reason you take the buck of a lifetime next season.

Deer Habitat And Hunting Tactics

All season long, Don Taylor had hunted a trophy 10-point that fooled him three times the year before.

I was confident at the beginning of the season that I had a trophy buck to hunt, which was something few hunters knew about the property in which they were hunting. I was able to deliberately lay out strategies for taking the trophy deer. But each time I saw the deer, the animal darted into thick cover before I could get off a shot. However, at least I had the experience of hunting a trophy.

Once the season was over, and intense hunting pressure was no longer present, I went back into the woods to find where the trophy deer had been hiding. I walked about 50 yards into a thicket along the route I thought the buck had traveled when I suddenly discovered him -or at least what was left of him. The deer either had been shot or had fought with another deer and lost, because his massive antlers lay in a heap on the edge of his decaying carcass. Perhaps someone on the adjoining property line shot the deer and either didn't know he had hit the animal or failed to follow up his shot.

Bob Zaiglin is a wildlife biologist who has done extensive research in managing and hunting trophy whitetail deer. A nationally- recognized expert for his rattling and calling techniques, Zaiglin is the wildlife manager for Harrison, Ltd.

Nothing is worse after the season than finding that the buck you've been hunting is dead.

But no matter what the reason, I knew my trophy buck was gone. I also realized I'd have to search diligently the next year to locate an animal in his trophy class.

Post-season scouting gives you an idea of the deer you'll be able to hunt in the upcoming season. If you know where a trophy buck is, then post-season scouting often will tell you whether the deer has made it through another season or not. Even if you don't spot the deer, you may find his shed antlers.

You may also see a trophy on your property after deer season is over. Deer learn to retreat from hunting pressure, and two to three weeks after the season is over, deer will often come out of their hideouts. They realize the danger from hunters is gone. By scouting after the season, you more likely will see where the deer have been hiding throughout hunting season and whether or not the animals still are on the land you hunt.

Scouting after the season also informs you of the amount of browse damage, which helps dictate whether or not you need to provide more food for the deer for the coming season. If the honeysuckle patches and greenbriar patches are eaten down, then you know the deer have just about exhausted all available food.

You may need to plant more greenfields and/or fertilize the existing briar patches and honeysuckle patches. Adding fertilizer to natural wild plants will increase their foliage, which also increases the amount of available food for deer. If the greenfields are eaten down almost to the ground, then the deer must have more food to get through the winter. However, if the greenfields are still lush in February and March, then you can assume enough food is present to carry the deer through the winter.

In late winter after deer season, when most of the foliage is gone from the trees and bushes, the hunter has an ideal opportunity to scout thick cover and out-of-the-way places that may have been difficult or almost impossible to get to earlier in the season. You can pass through easier to cut shooting lanes before the spring green-up and while the weather is still cool.

One of the most difficult tasks a sportsman has to perform is to test different hunting techniques during the season. Most of us prefer to go with proven tactics when our chances are good for bagging a buck. However, during the off-season, an outdoorsman can scout and locate deer. Then he can enter the woods with rattling horns, deer calls, scents and lures and test the effectiveness of these hunting methods while the rut is still happening. Also he can study rutting behavior and learn how both bucks and does interact during the rut. He can then use his camera to hunt instead of his gun.

Understanding Where Others Hunt

Bob Sheppard likes to scout after deer season to learn where the other hunters may have been hunting on the property.

If you have a reputation as a deer hunter, and you've taken several nice bucks, the folks on your hunting lease or on the same property you hunt will attempt to learn where you're hunting and put their treestands where your treestands are. Usually these hunters don't consider the wind or any other factor that makes a particular site a good place to hunt only on certain days. They'll foul up the area where you're hunting if they know where you are.

Shed antlers after the season will tell you the size of bucks you'll have to hunt the following season, and often, the number of trophy bucks

Since very few hunters scout after the season, I can go into the woods and find the best spots to hunt when no one else is in the woods. I also can learn how to get to these places unseen by other hunters. I can move into areas I won't walk in during hunting season for fear someone else will see where I'm going and possibly walk to that region with the wrong wind condition and spook the deer I'm trying to take. After the season, I can scout without being scouted myself by other hunters.

Scouting after the season allows you to study rutting behavior.

I also scout after the season to find out where other sportsmen's stands are and how they've been hunting. Although I've placed stands at sites that I'm confident will produce a buck, I may never see a buck at that place all season long. Then when the season is over, and I'm reconnoitering the area, I may discover a treestand 100 yards upwind from where I've been hunting.

Generally, once you've learned where hunters have hunted the past season, you can accurately predict where they'll be hunting the next season. Hunters, like deer, are creatures of habit. They most often will hunt from the same treestand sites or in the near where they've hunted in previous seasons.

When I know where other sportsmen will be hunting, I, like the deer, try to avoid the avoid the hunters. Most sportsmen leave their treestands up after the season, and these are like red lights showing me where not to hunt.

Hunting deer is like putting together a jigsaw puzzle. The more parts of the puzzle you have, the quicker you can solve it. Post-season scouting

Finding trophy buck sheds like this at the end of the season can help you bag that same deer the following season.

is a valuable tool in learning about deer. The more you can understand about deer, their habitat, and their habits and what other sportsmen on your property are doing and how they're hunting, the sooner you'll be able to find and take your buck of a lifetime.

Looking For Sheds

Bob Zaiglin searches for shed antlers and hunts bucks without a gun when the season is over to compile the most complete information about the whereabouts of deer.

Hunting sheds helps you learn where deer are concentrated on any particular piece of property. Wherever you find the most sheds will be the regions where you will discover the most deer. Also sportsmen can pinpoint the corridors deer are using to enter agricultural fields to feed, water, and bed and the places where deer are hiding from hunting pressure.

By hunting sheds, a sportsman may find a rack that will score very high on the Boone and Crockett scale, and that buck may never even have been seen during hunting season. Once the hunter locates that trophy shed and decides to hunt that trophy buck the next season, he must realize he will have to let numbers of small bucks walk past him. But knowing a trophy buck is in an area helps a hunter concentrate his hunting time the next season in the general region where he's found the trophy's shed antler.

In the West, I find many sheds around watering holes and along fence lines. Many times when deer are jumping fences, they'll knock their antlers off. A hunter can try to find travel trails between feeding and bedding areas along fences where he locates drops.

Although each of these places are easy spots to discover sheds, to locate the shed antlers of trophy bucks, you must look for them in the thicker spots. One of the problems with finding big sheds in heavy cover is that rodents are more abundant in thick areas and will consume those antlers at a rapid rate after the deer have shed them.

The dream of most shed hunters is to find a matched pair of trophy antlers, but very rarely do deer shed both antlers at the same time and in the same place.

Last year, I found for the first time more than two sets of matching antlers; I actually located five sets of matched antlers. I'm not sure why finding both antlers off the same deer is uncommon, but I guess that antler shedding and the casting of antlers could be related to nutrition. A deer with a good nutrition level holds his antlers longer than a deer that is deprived of good food.

40

Discovering dead deer in the woods after the season is an important piece of information for the hunter to have.

Last year our ranch had good nutrition. But after hunting season, the lands I managed went into a drought. The deer were somewhat deprived nutritionally and they shed their antlers more quickly. At least this is my best guess why I found more sets of antlers together after this past season.

Locating Dead Deer

Zaiglin also discovered some dead trophy deer while hunting sheds.

Last season, I picked up both sides of a 14-point buck that scored 176 points non-typical on the Boone and Crockett scale. A shed hunter will find these dead deer include not only deer that may have been wounded during hunting season, but also some deer that have died of natural causes. Remember you're hunting sheds after the rut. During the rut in regions with big deer, the trophy bucks usually will be beaten up badly during mating season. They may have to fight frequently, and the bigger, dominant buck must fight more often to prove his dominance.

These big old bucks are not invincible. They may develop an infection after being pierced by the antler of a rival. In this weakened condition, they can be attacked and killed by predators.

A buck can lose as much as 25 percent of his body weight during the rut, which is also the time of the year in many areas of the country when the snowfalls are the heaviest. After deer season in inclement weather, deer will concentrate heavily around food sources. In many regions of the country, farmers and landowners must feed deer so they can survive. In the brush country of South Texas after the rut, the land tends to get dry.

Some deer, especially trophy deer, simply die of old age, having escaped hunting pressure through the years. Too, deer are accident prone. Sometimes they'll run into a tree and kill themselves or become hung up on fences and die. Heat affects deer adversely as does drought, and whitetails are susceptible to various parasites and diseases. The main reason you find dead deer when hunting sheds is because you are in the woods at the time they generally die off.

Determining The Condition Of The Herd

Zaiglin believes the best time to lease land or to look for a place to hunt is after the rut.

If a hunter is considering leasing a particular piece of property and wants to know the condition of the deer on the land, he should be able to walk over the lease and find sheds. If he doesn't discover any sheds, then he must question how many deer are on the lease. The same is true of public lands. If public lands are available but you aren't sure what the condition of the deerherd is on those lands, then walk the land after the season, and search for sheds.

Sheds will tell sportsmen how well the deer management program is working. For instance, if your hunting club is attempting to produce numbers of bucks, and your members don't find very many sheds, then something is wrong in your deer management program. Sheds will also tell you the size of bucks you have on the property and the general condition of those bucks.

On the Harrison ranches I manage, we collect all the sheds we discover every year and we measure them. Although the data doesn't give us any age criteria, it does give us a bio mass of antlers. We can tell by the volume of antlers we pick up whether we have a number of bucks or a few bucks and whether we have little or big bucks.

Finding small sheds like these helps the hunter to know what kind of deer he can expect to take during the upcoming season.

I've personally been collecting and weighing sheds for years. I'm attempting to evaluate from the sheds whether we've had a good year, a great year or an average year for antler development on the properties we manage. The sheds allow us to determine what size bucks are available for the hunter the upcoming year. If we find numbers of small, scrappy antlers, then we can project that hunters may not bag very many large trophies. But if we locate some quality racks, we'll know our hunters the following year can expect to harvest some trophy bucks. So collecting sheds helps the sportsman establish reasonable expectations of the upcoming buck harvest.

The odds of bagging that trophy buck are best for the hunter who makes the commitment to hunt deer all year long.

Bass fishermen have learned that bass usually are in only 10 percent of a lake's area. Deer follow much the same pattern in the woods. Shed hunters quickly will learn where their chances are best on any piece of property to find a deer.

Locked Horns

Bob Zaiglin has found one of the most discouraging sights in nature - two bucks with antlers locked in combat and both deer dead.

When a hunter discovers two locked racks, he knows that the sex ratio of the deer herd is probably approximately one buck for each doe, because bucks fight more and therefore lock horns more often when there are fewer does.

Finding two bucks locked in combat was thought to be very uncommon in past years. However, several years ago we had 15 bucks radio-collared on the Harrison's 100,000-acre Catarina Ranch. Out of those 15 bucks, one of those radio-collared bucks locked up with another deer.

This past year, we found two sets or four bucks that locked antlers - one pair in December and the other in February. These bucks were a tremendous size. Two of these deer had racks that scored close to 170 points on the Boone and Crockett scale.

Becoming A Year Round Hunter

Bob Zaiglin believes the sportsman who wants to become a trophy hunter and consistently take big deer must learn to hunt all year long and carry his gun into the woods only during hunting season.

Not enough time is available during hunting season in most states for a trophy hunter to unravel the mysteries of the big bucks. Even if the outdoorsman does determine what the deer in his area are doing, the season may be over before he has a chance to intercept a buck in the woods. Deer are not that smart, but they have learned to avoid hunters.

On any given piece of land, a certain few bucks will continually escape hunters. These deer seem to have a sixth sense about how to avoid them. Unless a sportsman is willing to hunt trophy bucks all year long, he not only may never find a trophy buck to hunt, but also he'll never develop a strategy for taking that deer.

The odds of bagging that trophy buck are best for the hunter who makes the commitment to hunt deer all year long. Shed hunting is an integral part of trophy buck hunting for outdoorsmen who understand what sheds mean, where to look for the sheds, and what to do after finding them.

CHAPTER 4

HOW WIND AFFECTS BUCKS
With Dr. Robert Sheppard

I WAS HUNTING a narrow strip of woods between a cleared field and a river. The area I was hunting was about 60 yards wide and about 400 yards long and separated two large hardwood bottoms. That small strip of woods ran north and south, and the only way to approach the land without having my scent mess up my hunting site was in from the west, which was the river side, or the east, which was the field side.

On this particular morning, I walked into this strip of woods from the east with a west wind in my face. Any deer moving either south or north would not pick up my scent.

I got into my stand just at daylight and had been sitting for about an hour when I spotted a nice six point buck coming from the south side of the woods moving north. The deer walked to within 15 steps of me and never picked up my scent.

I let my arrow fly and struck the deer just behind the shoulder. Immediately he bounded away and over the side of the bank. I found him on the edge of the river. If the buck had smelled me, I never would have had the shot.

The deer's best defense against any predator is his nose. Many treestand hunters will tell you that a deer may be able to see you, he may walk up, look straight at you and then walk on past as if you don't exist, if he doesn't smell you.

This same group of hunters may tell you of instances where they've shot more than one arrow at the same deer, and he's never moved. But you rarely will find an instance when a deer has smelled a hunter and presented anything but a hindquarter shot. Many times a deer may be able to see you or hear you - but you still may be able to take your animal. However, if he smells you, I'll lay odds that you'll never get a shot.

How To Determine Wind Direction

I methodically check wind direction through several different methods before I finally enter my stand. The first thing I do every morning is to check my weather radio and listen to what the prediction for the wind direction is for that day.

Each day I hunt, the wind dictates the choice of stands I have. I will hunt only out of the stands that face into the wind. I have 10 to 20 stand sites in the woods, which means I have a stand I can hunt from, regardless of the wind direction, on any given day. Once I know the wind's direction, I begin to narrow down my choice of stands.

Another factor that is added to the final decision of where I will hunt is how much time has passed since I've visited these stand sites. The two stand sites that I have hunted from the least in recent weeks will be my choice for the morning hunt. By depending on the wind, I have narrowed my choices from 20 sites to two.

But once I decide which stand I will hunt out of due to the prevailing wind, I don't turn my brain off. When I get into my car and head for the woods, I observe every chimney I pass. I have my compass on the front seat of the car and check the direction of the chimney smoke. If every chimney has its smoke blowing in a different direction during the 15 mile drive between my house and the woods, then I begin to wonder if I'm hunting on a day when the wind will be variable and unpredictable and/or if there are thermals affecting the air current.

By the time I reach the woods, if I determine that the wind is variable and will not be blowing consistently from one direction, then I spend my day scouting instead of hunting. Although many hunters will continue with their hunt plans and disregard the wind, to be successful I must hunt as the wind dictates. Since 80 percent of my time in the woods is spent scouting, selecting stand sites and cutting shooting lanes, and only 20 percent of my time actually is spent in a tree, I never view the days with variable winds as wasted hunting time.

Just before I get to the area I plan to hunt, I stop my car in a region that has a wide open field on both sides of the road. I don't want any trees or obstructions to create additional wind turbulence. I get out of the car and take one of my broadheads with a piece of string tied to it, hold it out and

From the wind, a buck can pick up human odor which will alert him to the hunter's presence.

see in which direction the wind pushes the string. Then I check the wind with my compass to make sure it is still blowing in the same direction that I have heard on the weather radio and have seen blowing from the chimneys.

If the wind direction is still constant, then I go ahead and walk through the woods to the stand I have planned to hunt from that day. As I approach the treestand, I also am conscious that I am walking into the wind and not with the wind at my back. Once I arrive at my stand and get into the tree, I continue to observe the string tied to the end of my broadhead or my gun barrel and my compass. Any time the wind changes direction or the air movement varies, the string will indicate in which direction way my scent is being blown.

What Are Thermals

Wind, which is one form of air movement, is generally directional to points on the compass. But thermals are usually upward or downward air

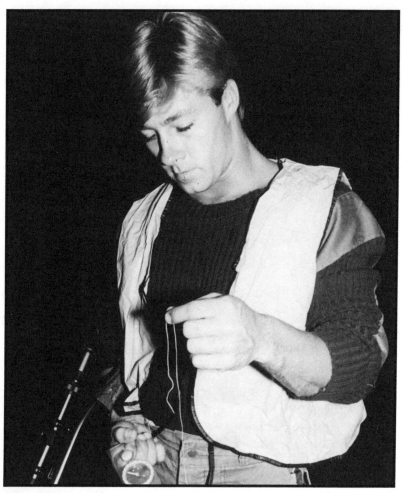

Before entering the woods, check wind direction with a string and compass.

movements. The effects of thermals are well known to most sportsmen in mountainous regions. However, outdoorsmen who hunt more flat terrains don't give much thought to them.

When hunting on the side of a mountain that is two miles from the bottom to the top, most hunters realize they want to be hunting the top side of the mountain in the morning when the thermals cause the air at the bottom to rise to the top. In the afternoon, they prefer to hunt at the bottom of the mountain, when the thermals will cause the air at the top to drift to

If you understand thermals, you can often hunt a hotspot with the wind blowing from the wrong direction.

the bottom. The general upward drift of air in the morning will take the hunter's scent up and away from the deer, and the general downward movement of the air in the afternoon will keep the hunter's scent close to the ground and away from the deer.

The flatland hunter has to deal with thermals as the mountain hunter does, but the thermals aren't as obvious. When a hunter goes to his stand early in the afternoon with little or no wind, his scent will be forced straight down the tree and spread out in all directions. For deer to come within shooting range and not smell a hunter under these conditions is almost impossible.

Another unfavorable condition for a hunter in search of a buck is being in a treestand late in the afternoon during a rain with no wind when the fog is pushed close to the ground. This weather condition will make your scent hug close to the ground. The same situation prevails in any type of rainy

If you don't understand the wind and its effect on deer, then this may be the shot you most often will get.

weather that lasts all day with no wind. During those times, the best thing to do is either scout, try and stalk a deer or go home.

One of my best tactics for hunting during no-win situations is to not go to my stand until 30 minutes before dark. I want to spend as little time as possible in that stand under these conditions, since the longer I sit in the stand, the more time I give my scent to spread all over the area.

A hunter can use thermals to his advantage if the wind is slight and moving five miles an hour or less. In the morning, you often can hunt from a stand with the wind at your back. With a slow wind and a rising thermal, your scent will be carried upwards above the deer. Then you can hunt out of a stand even if the wind is blowing in the wrong direction.

I proved this point to myself one season. I was in my treestand early one morning and spotted a fine eight point buck. The deer would have scored 110 or 120 points on the Boone & Crockett scale. I already could visualize him mounted on my den wall. But since I saw him coming from downwind, I felt sure he would pick up my scent. However, the weather conditions were right. The time was early morning and only a very slight breeze was present, which meant my scent was rising.

I watched the big buck come under my scent. Right at the point he should have winded me, he didn't. He continued to move into the zone where there was no doubt he would have winded me except that the rising thermal and the slight wind carried my scent over his head. At 20 yards, I drew and released my arrow. However, not only was I lucky that day - the deer was too. I missed, and the deer went on his way.

If you understand thermals, sometimes you can hunt even when the wind direction may carry your scent to the deer. To know what is going on with thermals when you are in the treestand, tie a small piece of string onto the end of your broadhead or gun barrel. In the morning, thermals will cause the thread to lift up and settle back down. In the late evening, the thread will hang straight down if there is no wind.

Although I'm a cardiologist and totally against smoking, you can test this theory by lighting a cigarette in late afternoon with no wind and watching the smoke settle to the ground. Early in the morning, you can see the smoke rise, even with no wind. The way the cigarette smoke moves is the same way your scent travels.

Using The Wind to Your Advantage

A strong, blowing wind and a driving rain is often a definite advantage to successful hunting.

One morning I went to my stand when the wind was at 20 knots, and a driving rain was falling. On the way, I spotted a buck a half mile away standing in a bean field. I had three options for trying to take the deer. I could walk straight across the bean field and spook the buck for sure. I could circle upwind, and he would pick up my scent. Or I could make the 1-1/2-mile hike downwind below the deer and try and come up behind him.

Although the stalk would be longer and a greater chance existed for him to see and hear me, the stalk was the only chance I would have. With this option, I also knew the deer wouldn't be able to smell me because the rain was falling so hard and the wind was really blowing. Any movement sounds would be masked by the storm. Everything in the woods was moving, and I would fit in naturally as I moved through the forest.

The buck was about 50 yards away facing the wind. For some unknown reason, he turned and walked right into the woods where I was and presented a 20 yard target. I bagged him.

In my opinion, hunting with a favorable wind is the most critical ingredient to bagging a buck once you have determined in what area the deer probably is.

CHAPTER 5

BAG A BUCK THROUGH HIS STOMACH
With Dr. Keith Causey

THREE ELEMENTS CAUSE deer to move - fear, sex and food. Once the hunter understands these three elements, he can predict deer movement more effectively and determine where and when a deer will show up.

Fear usually plays a role in deer movement when hunter pressure is intense. Sex influences deer movement during the rut. However, every morning when a deer wakes up, he must decide what he is going to eat for breakfast. Deer usually will eat something almost every day. Therefore, a food supply, as it relates to deer, may be the most dependable ingredient for harvest success.

Deer are so widespread across the United States that they have learned to adapt to a broad range of habitat, including the prairie grasses of Texas and Kansas, the coniferous forests of the West and New England, and the southern forests. We know these animals are very tolerant of whatever conditions the environment makes available to them. Because these animals are so adaptable, they can and will eat virtually all the food sources that are available to them.

Some years ago, I learned and understood the effect that the acorn of the white oak tree had on deer in a region. I found a big oak tree deep in the swamps. Underneath the tree it looked as though a kindergarten class had a party there -with the leaves all disturbed.

Paths went in several directions, and the spot was recognizable from 50 or more yards away because of the way the leaves were disturbed. Deer droppings and a bed of half acorn shells lay on the groun. Even a hunter

Dr. Keith Causey has been a wildlife researcher for more than 20 years at Auburn University. An avid deer hunter, Causey brings new scientific hunting information to the hunting fraternity each year.

with very little woods experience would have been able to determine that this was a deer hotspot.

The first afternoon I took a stand 50 yards from the tree, a fat six point came in to feed on the acorns and fell to my rifle. I hunted the white oak tree for another two weeks and took two more spikes from under its branches before the acorns stopped falling from the tree and the deer quit coming into the area.

When you hunt in a region where deer season with bow and arrow begins October 15, and November 20 for guns, and runs through the last day of January, you can't depend on hunting over on one food source all season long. In many sections of the country, one particular food source may not last a week.

Deer seem to change from one preferred food to another within a 10-day to a two week period. Deer don't like to eat the same food over an extended time and soon tire of one particular food source. They enjoy variety in their diet because no one food source has all the nutrients they need for their bodies. But when you can find food that the deer are eating regularly, more than likely you have an excellent chance of bagging your buck.

Determining Deer's Preferred Foods

When we look more closely at why I was able to bag three bucks under the same white oak tree, we have to understand why the deer continued to show up in this particular place. The white oak at the time I was hunting was a preferred food of the whitetail deer.

Deer will pick, nibble, eat and browse on almost everything in the forest including all kinds of grasses, nuts and fruits. But like humans, some foods feel better in their mouths or taste better to them. The deer will take the choice parts of a plant maybe one month out of the year and ignore that plant the other 11 months.

In any given area, deer may have a half dozen foods they prefer over others. For instance, deer in my part of the country like oak seedlings and the ash group of trees better than they do hickory or pine seedlings. Also there are seasonal preferences for foods like muscadines, persimmons and other fruits that occur once a year.

The deer's preferred foods are much like the dessert part of his meal. Many times the deer will walk a considerable distance to find that dessert. However, even when you know what the deer's chosen food is during the time you plan to hunt, you cannot be certain that you'll concentrate the animals close enough to your stand to take a shot. To hunt over a preferred food source, that food has to be in short supply in the specific region where you are hunting. Then it will draw deer to it from the surrounding geographical region.

For instance, the white oak tree I hunted was the only one within about 1-1/2 miles. Most of the deer came to that tree to get the white oak acorns during the time the tree was dropping the acorns. When the acorns ceased to fall, the deer quit coming.

Besides a deer's preferred food changing throughout the year, the favorite food in one region for a certain group of deer may not be a favorite food in another area for another group of deer.

One veteran hunter told me that on the West side of the state during the early fall, the deer prefer white oak acorns and turn their noses up at the red oaks, while on the other side of the state, the deer like the red oak acorns best.

57

Knowing what the deer's preferred food is during the time you plan to hunt him is a major key to success.

In many parts of the north, the deer's preferred food during hunting season may be apples from an orchard. Yet in other sections of the country where apples are few, the deer may select sumac or soybeans instead.

To learn which foods you can concentrate deer around, contact your state's game commission. Most states have a district biologist who is responsible for the game in each particular area. This wildlife specialist usually will know what the deer's favorite food is during each week of hunting season. He also can tell you how to recognize the preferred food and where you can find it. Hunters often waste thousands of hours scouting instead of contacting wildlife biologists in the area they plan to hunt before they enter the woods.

Once a sportsman learns the deer's preferred food, then he is ready to scout the woods and try to locate that food. When you find that preferred food, you should be able to tell from tracks, droppings and signs such as cracked acorn halves, nipped leaves or chewed branches, if the deer are utilizing that food source in the area you plan to hunt. Next, search for either a large concentration of that particular food source that will draw the deer into the food or an area that has very little of the deer's preferred food.

Changes in nature may also change a deer's preferred food. Droughts, floods and other natural calamities interrupt the growth patterns of a specific food source and affect what the deer eat. Deer can determine the best and most nutritious food available in a given area. If one year the soil type in a region is basically poor, and the browse it produces is also poor, deer will gravitate toward a well-fertilized greenfield that is producing better food than they can locate in the woods.

Last season, the acorn crop failed on the lease I hunt, which changed our traditional hunting pattern. Instead of hunting the acorn flats as we had for many years, the men I hunted with had to locate a different food source to hunt over.

As we scouted the woods, we discovered that poke sallet had grown along many of the logging trails, especially the new ones. Where we found the poke sallet, we also located plenty of deer trails. Most of the poke sallet leaves were nipped off at the stems. As we continued to watch the poke sallet, we found that whenever there was even a thumb-sized leaf coming out from the stems, the deer nipped these tender greens. On opening day, each of us located different logging roads with poke sallet on them where we took stands. All of us shot deer.

The deer's feeding habits had changed because of the failing acorn crop. Even though the deer's preferred food historically was acorns, if we had not scouted before the season, discovered that the acorn crop had failed and then located a new food source, our opening day hunt would have been a disaster.

When The Pressure Is On

Even though the hunger pains in a deer's stomach direct him toward a preferred food source, the deer does not lose his instincts. In areas where the hunting pressure is high, especially around a favorite food source like a greenfield or an agricultural crop, the deer may show up for the first day or two. Then they may vanish. A keen observer soon will discover the deer are still utilizing the food in the field but are primarily coming at night.

You can continue to hunt deer around a greenfield or agricultural crops when hunting pressure is high. Follow the trail away from the field into the woods. Try and intercept the deer either early or late as he comes to or goes away from the field where he is feeding. Reduce the amount of

A soybean field like this one can concentrate deer if the beans are the deerherd's preferred food.

hunting pressure on the particular field a group of deer are using. If you and your hunting companions have several fields to hunt, don't allow hunting on all the fields all the time. Save a few fields for later on in the season. By reducing the amount of hunting pressure on a particular field, you often can keep the deer feeding there all season long.

Look for an alternate food source. If intense hunting pressure is exerted on a particular food source, the animal may change its feeding patterns and start feeding on an alternate type of food.

Inclement weather can cause deer to change their preferred food source.

When The Food Is Gone

If high concentrations of deer live in the region you hunt, they may devour all the preferred deer food in a very short time. Oftentimes, inclement weather may destroy the food source you have been hunting over. Or, hunting pressure may cause the deer to leave their preferred food source and search out another type of food. When this happens, the hunter who adjusts quickly to the deer's changing feeding patterns will be the sportsman most likely to take a buck.

When deer stop utilizing one food source, they don't quit eating. The hunter who can determine what type of food the deer seem to prefer later in the season will be able to more consistently predict where a deer will show up.

For instance, in the southern part of the country where I live, deer will begin feeding on agricultural crops and other browse during late summer and fall. Then when the crops are harvested and the acorns begin to fall, the animals usually will feed on acorns or something like poke sallet in the late season. After that food is depleted, deer generally will start concentrating on greenfields or blackberry bushes. During the cold, winter months, greenbriar (smilax) most often will be their preferred food.

Any hunter who can tell when the deer leave one food source and go to another usually will have at least a week or two head start at taking a buck before other outdoorsmen who are still hunting over the abandoned food source.

When Snow And Water Covers The Land

During the fall and winter, when rains and snow often cover the ground, much of the deer food will be inaccessible to the animals. However, once again the deer don't stop eating. They change their feeding patterns and sometimes the foods on which they are relying.

When the snow comes, the deer will begin to browse on small twigs and leaves that are above the snow. If the rains cause flooding, the deer will look for food on high ground. But what some hunters fail to realize is that the deer may feed out in water.

In many river bottom swamps, after the acorns have fallen and the land becomes flooded, the acorns will float to the surface. Depending on the water's current, the acorns may be lying right on top of the water for the deer to eat. I've seen deer along a flood plain wading in chest-deep water, picking up the acorns out of the water and feeding on them.

A current coming into a flooded hardwood bottom will cause the acorns to float to the surface and collect along the edge of the water or in pockets near the back of the flooded land. Wherever the acorns float to and concentrate is where you can expect to find high concentrations of deer. Sometimes the acorns and the deer will collect in unusual places.

Once I found an excellent stand where I took two fine bucks. The acorns from the hardwood bottom had floated up to the surface. As the water came into the swamp, the acorns were washed into a pine forest about 1/4-mile from the bottom. Although normally the deer would have nothing to eat in the pine forest, the water brought the acorns to the pines, which also drew the deer and made the hunting productive.

If you remember that deer have to eat, and if you know what they prefer to eat, where the food source is found and whether or not that preferred food is in relatively short supply, then locating deer to hunt can be simple. The hunter who gleans information from wildlife biologists, learns where the plants, trees, shrubs, fruits and nuts that the deer like to eat are located and watches for the deer to change from one feeding pattern to another will increase his chances of success this season.

One of the best ways to take a buck this year is to learn what the deer is putting in his stomach. Then you will know where you have to be to take him.

CHAPTER 6

USING THE FEAR FACTOR
With Dr. Keith Causey

THE OLD, WIDE-ANTLERED buck had been spotted by several hunters for two or three years running. But all that was seen were his white tail and his broad antlers as he escaped. The buck was smart. He seemed to be able to read every move the hunters made and anticipated each step they took. The size of the buck's antlers proved his wisdom.

However, big deer and older deer are not without their Achilles' heels. They can be patterned. Once you know what makes deer move and why and where the deer moves, you can take him.

This majestic buck, which always was heading in the opposite direction from the hunters, was seen only when hunters were entering the woods. Finally one day my friend, Richard Sharp, laid a game plan to try and outsmart the wily whitetail.

He got up at 3:00 A.M., came in behind the area where the deer usually was seen and waited for the buck to escape. Sharp's game plan was a can't-miss scheme to take the old buck as he escaped from hunting pressure. But Sharp overlooked a critical ingredient in mastering an old buck - the wind direction. The wind that morning was coming from Sharp's back, and he failed to realize his scent was being swept into the section through which he expected the big buck to come.

That same morning, Jimmy Shipman and I also hunted the big buck. We eased into the woods where we thought the deer might be. Since Sharp had the deer's retreat cut off, we felt we could drive the deer in his direction so he could take it.

Knowing how a big buck reacts to the fear factor will help you to locate him.

What we did not know was that as the wind brought Sharp's scent into the deer's range, and we approached from the opposite direction, the big buck buried deep into the thickest cover available.

I walked into a briar thicket hoping to jump up a smaller deer. All of a sudden the sky was filled with ivory-colored antlers and the wide, brown back of a magnificent buck. I fired in the center of the deer's back. The 00 buckshot broke the animal's back and drove him to the ground. He was a trophy - the deer of a lifetime.

Where The Big Bucks Stay

Hunt club members who regularly hunt the same 2,000 acres every weekend and several days through the week, sometimes assume the

Hunting with a favorable wind can help you get a shot like this.

hunting pressure will drive big deer out of a region. But this assumption can be incorrect.

Studies using radio telemetry on deer indicate that the whitetail usually spends his lifetime within one square mile. Of course there are exceptions to this rule. But most of the time, a deer will not leave his home range.

Larry Marchinton, of the University of Georgia, attempted to drive deer out of their home ranges by constantly harassing them with dogs. Of all the deer that Marchinton studied, only one animal left its home range and did not return.

What Deer Fear Most About Man

What deer fear more than any other thing is man's odor. Once deer are able to make a sight association with man's odor and the form of a man, one of two things happens. They either can become adjusted to the sight of men and lose their fear of them or, if the deer are constantly harassed by humans, they will learn to panic at the sight of man, whether or not they smell him. The hunter trains the deer to fear him.

Whitetail fawns learn to fear man from the doe, which transfers these signals to her fawn so that it knows what to run from and what to fear. I feel that, as well as being a learned response, human odor may release a natural fear response in deer.

Although no way exists to monitor the intelligence or thought processes of a deer, we can assume that the more human contact the animal has, the more adept he becomes at avoiding human encounters. This may explain why so many 1-1/2-year old animals are taken each year in deer harvest, and why the older deer are less likely to be killed. The deer that are able to survive past 1-1/2-years of age have to be better at escaping humans by smelling their scent and seeing them in the woods than the younger deer are.

This scientific information gives outdoorsmen two options for taking trophy deer. A hunter either can use the fear response of human odor and human sight to drive the deer to another hunter, or he can eliminate human odor and the sight of a human from the deer's senses.

To eliminate human odor, some hunters utilize masking scents. These are not lures or attractants but actually attempts to mask human odor with an odor that is familiar to the deer. However, a masking scent is most effective when it is put on the bottoms of shoes or boots when entering the woods and used in conjunction with a favorable wind.

By talking to other hunters, you can learn where most of them will be hunting during deer season.

The best way to eliminate human odor is to hunt with the wind in your face so the deer approaches your stand from downwind. To do that you must know from which direction the deer would be walking on the day you plan to hunt. If the wind is wrong for the stand you have picked, do not hunt from that stand that day to avoid having the deer pick up your odor and, possibly prevent it from coming into the region. Hunting with a favorable wind may be one of the most overlooked keys to taking trophy bucks.

The second requirement for bagging older, bigger deer is to disguise the human form. This is one of the reasons that treestands are so effective - the hunter is above the deer's eye level. However, if you are hunting in a region where outdoorsmen historically have hunted from treestands, then the deer may have been trained to look into the trees for sportsmen. Using back cover is critical to your success, and the type of tree selected is important. Again, if the hunter does not allow the deer to make visual contact with him, he will be more likely to bag an older, bigger buck than would the sportsman the deer can see moving or standing in the woods.

Effects Of Hunting Pressure

Hunting pressure makes deer more secretive. Many times a great deal of hunting pressure will cause animals to become nocturnal. If you are hunting in an area with high hunter pressure, the deer will use the best escape cover possible to get away from the hunter.

Escape cover may not always be dense undergrowth. In certain parts of Louisiana, biologists have had reports where just the opposite appears to be true. The deer have been observed moving out into the middle of cotton fields where they stay bedded down sometimes as far as half a mile away from the nearest woodline. These deer realize the hunters are in the woods, not in the fields. This very sparse cover is a safe haven to these deer.

Louisiana hunters never figured out where the deer were. The deer were spotted by pilots in light aircraft who remarked about the many big bucks they had seen in the fields. Evidently the deer gave up heavy cover for sparse cover if they could avoid hunters.

To take trophy deer, a wise hunter will study how other hunters hunt, just as he also studies the deer's movement patterns. Before determininng where the buck should be when he is frightened, you have to first know where the hunter who causes this fear response will show up.

To properly pattern deer and their response to fear, you must determine what types of cover draw the most hunters. Hunters tend to hunt traditional places. This may be the deepest part of the woods or an area where hunters historically have seen deer. To take trophy deer, decide where the least numbers of hunters are likely to show up, which should be some of the best areas to take an older, smarter buck. You may very well luck up on a trophy animal bedded down in an unlikely place.

Hunters may be surprised at some of the areas where trophy deer hide out during daylight hours to avoid hunting pressure. One of the spots may be beside a rural residence with plenty of human activity, noise and a yard full of dogs. A smart buck may move to within rock throwing distance of a rural home and bed down during daylight hours, because he realizes this area is where the fewest hunters are likely to show up.

Aerial photos not only will help you determine where hunters hunt but also will give you an idea of where trophy bucks have to be to avoid hunting pressure.

Another unlikely place to find trophy deer during daylight hours when there is much hunting pressure is beside a major road. The hunters usually will drive past this area to get to the woods.

Most hunters often prefer to go to the backside of the property to hunt, and over the years, the mature, knowledgeable animals learn where the majority of the hunters are during hunting season. They will avoid these regions and move into the fringe places that the hunter rarely visits.

To use the fear factor as a tool to find trophy bucks, you have to pattern the other hunters in your hunting region as well as the game. One of the best ways is to utilize an aerial photo of the region you plan to hunt. Mark the roads in red, then use paper arrows to point out the direction of the hunters' movements from the roads into the areas that are hunted the most.

Once you determine hunter flow on the map, the place where the least amount of hunter pressure occurs will become apparent. If you use the same map for several years and plot the movement of hunters during several seasons, you will understand the deer soon see where the trophy animals have to go to survive. By utilizing your map, you will be able to spend most of your hunting season in the areas with the least amount of hunting pressure. The likelihood of your taking and seeing trophy bucks will increase drastically.

CHAPTER 7

UTILIZING TREESTANDS PRODUCTIVELY

THE WIND WAS HOWLING, the rain was coming down, and I was praying my treestand wouldn't turn loose from where I had attached it. As I sat 15 feet up in the beech tree riding out the storm, I asked myself, "What am I doing here? I don't have any reason in the world to believe a deer will pass this way."

"Since my shooting glove is wet, the bowstring probably will slide off my fingers. I'm freezing to death. With the wind blowing like it is, most likely I'll fall out of the tree if I stand to shoot. The only reason I've put a treestand here anyway is because a few acorns have fallen from nearby trees. But plenty of acorns are everywhere in these woods."

"I'm smarter than this. I ought to get down out of this tree, go back to the warm lodge and wait until a nicer day to hunt. Surely I can find a better place to put my treestand than just anywhere in the woods on a rainy day."

Realizing the wisdom of what my inner voice was telling me, I left the woods and decided to wait for a better day for deer hunting. But more importantly, I determined I would select a more productive spot to place my treestand the next time.

To be a master of deer hunting, you must understand the elements required for the best treestand placement and the most productive treestand hunting.

Which Type Of Treestand

When you choose the best treestand for your style of deer hunting, you must consider many factors. Picking the right treestand is much like attempting to select the most beautiful girl in a beauty contest. Although the first four finishers will be happy, the rest of the contestants will be mad. Usually the way one person measures beauty is different from the standards others may use.

Here's the particular types of stands I prefer and the reasons they're my favorites. You must make up your own mind which is the best for you. The masters of deer hunting consider and try many different options and tactics before choosing the ones that work best for them.

Ladder Type Stand

The ladder type stand that can be either chained on, strapped on or, in some other way, fastened to the side of a tree is my favorite. The reasons for my choice are simple. Ladder stands are relatively safe to climb (at least as safe as any treestand) and comfortable to sit in, and allow you to get into or come out of the stand making a minimum of noise. This noise factor is one of the key determinants why I like a ladder stand better than all other types.

It does have one disadvantage, however. The ladder stand is not very portable and moving it is often a problem. But because very little noise is made getting into and out of the stand, it is a superior hunting platform.

Lock-On-Limb Stand

Although this kind of stand can be portable, I believe it is better to put this stand on a tree and leave it. Then you climb in or out of it with either screw- in or strap-on steps. Once this type of stand is put up, and the steps are attached to the tree, you can move in and out of it much quicker, easier and quieter than you can with the climbing stands.

The lock-on-limb stand has the disadvantage of not being very portable. Climbing strap-on or screw-in type steps is not as easy or as comfortable as with a ladder type stand. Also, quite a bit of work is involved in putting these stands up and in taking them down. But again, the lack of noise you create getting into this style of stand is why it's my second-favorite choice.

Climbing Stand

Most of us who have been deer hunting for awhile have been up and down trees utilizing climbing type stands. These portable stands offer you much more mobility than either the ladder or the lock-on-limb stand and steps do.

The portable treestand allows the hunter to safely take a stand anywhere he finds deer signs and trees to climb.

In my opinion, however, the climbing stand is very noisy as you climb in and out of it. It also doesn't seem to provide as much security as the ladder and lock-on-limb type stands do.

Hunters often assume that having a portable stand means they need to move it numerous times to hunt effectively rather than leave the stands in the woods like the ladder or lock on limb stands. But the noise factor is the reason I list the climbing stand as my least preferred.

A ladder stand might be most effective in a bottleneck area where deer move frequently throughout the year.

Treestand Safety

An accurate statement is probably that the only people who don't fall out of treestands are the ones who don't use them. I'm not saying treestands are unsafe; many hunters who fall out of them have been sleeping in their stands without utilizing an essential piece of equipment - a safety belt.

But sooner or later, you have to decide whether or not you want to hunt from a treestand. I will hunt from a treestand because I think it's one of the most effective ways to bag a whitetail. However, I won't climb too high off the ground. Then, even if I do fall, the chance of getting hurt is minimized.

It's important that hunters wear safety belts at all times. Be very careful when climbing into and out of your stand, which is frequently when many accidents occur. One of the most successful treestand hunters I know reduces his chances for accidents by using a safety belt and spending most of his time standing. He believes that by standing he stays more alert, more intent on hunting, more prepared for taking a shot and is less likely to have an accident. If he becomes fatigued, he will sit down for five or ten minutes to take a break and then stand and hunt again for 30 to 45 minutes. Anyone who hunts from a treestand should be safety conscious by anticipating the hazards that being suspended in the air can bring.

Placing Your Treestand

When I was sitting in my treestand in the middle of the rainstorm, I had discounted completely the major reason for hunting from a treestand - placing it in the best area of the woods to try and bag a deer. I also had not paid attention to the weather or the wind direction.

What constitutes a productive place to put a treestand? Here are some ideas successful hunters use:

      ... locate an area where the deer are feeding

      ... find a hot scraping region where the deer want to breed

      ... discover a trail that the deer are using heavily

      ... locate a creek crossing

      ... find a funnel area

      ... set up an escape route

      ... pick the spot that provides the best opportunity for taking a deer.

Let's examine each of these sites to learn why they are effective.

Feeding Areas

Deer feed on many different types of grasses, bushes and nuts. Although the whitetail is a browser, he usually prefers one food source. Find a particular food source in short supply, and oftentimes that food source will concentrate the deer. Then you can set up your treestand close to the food source and have a better than average chance of bagging a deer. Remember to keep your stand a sufficient distance away from the food source so the deer doesn't see you when he comes in to feed.

A Hot Scrape

A hot scrape can be defined as one that has a well-used deer trail coming to it, a strong urine smell in the pawed-up ground and a limb hanging over the pawed-up ground that has been crunched by the deer. During the rut, and even before and after the rut, deer make many scrapes. But an active scrape usually holds a strong urine smell, is often in thick cover and has tracks leading to and from it.

Generally, the best site in which to set your stand is 30 to 50 yards downwind of a scrape. An older, smarter buck may come into a scraping area 20 to 30 yards downwind of the scrape to test the air for a doe close to the scrape. Not smelling the scent of a doe, he then may go on to his scrape and work it. If you put your treestand 30 to 50 yards below the scrape on the downwind side, your chances of taking the whitetail are greater.

Trails

The whitetail is a creature of habit that moves from one place to another as methodically as most of us go to and from the grocery store on certain days at specific times. To set up your treestand close to the best trail, look for a path in the woods that has tracks going both ways. Then you will know the deer are using this trail when they travel in either direction. More deer movement will be along this trail than a trail that has tracks leading only in one direction.

Creek Crossings

Most of the time, deer will cross a creek or a branch at the same point. A creek crossing where the water is more shallow than surrounding water or where the distance between the two banks is shorter is an excellent place to set up your treestand.

Funnel Areas

Deer will funnel between two types of habitat to get from one woodlot to another. For instance, if a large expanse of woods is divided by a narrow point where a field corners and a creek offers a barrier on the other side of the funnel, the woods between the corner of the field and the creek is a productive spot for a treestand. Most deer in both sections of the woods will prefer to walk through the funnel in that narrow neck of woods between the creek and the field, rather than swimming the creek or walking in the field.

Although funnel areas may be the best opportunity for taking a deer from a treestand, don't be concerned if you don't find trails in these funnel regions. Deer often meander through funnels rather than utilizing well-defined trails.

Without a treestand, the hunter has to stand on limbs, increasing his odds of falling by at least 150 percent.

Escape Routes

Deer have certain trails or routes they take to escape danger. When hunting pressure is heavy in a part of the woods, deer usually flee down escape trails to miss the hunters. Oftentimes these trails will be coming out of thick cover or will have tracks running in one direction away from the area where most of the hunters enter the woods. By getting into your treestand close to an escape route well before daylight, you may have the opportunity to bag your buck as he attempts to run from the other hunters entering the woods.

Best Spots

A deer hunter who is familiar with how to scout for deer often will find 10 to 20 good treestand sites in a half acre of woods. To be an effective treestand hunter, you must eliminate 19 of these stand sites and use the one that provides the best opportunity to take a deer on the day you plan to hunt.

Wind Effects

Another ingredient that helps any stand site is being on the best spot to hunt into the wind. Because the most effective treestand hunters are the ones who hunt from treestands in prime areas with a favorable wind, many of them use a multiple stand hunt plan.

The multiple stand concept requires you to have more than one stand in the woods on the day you plan to hunt. Some hunters have from five to 20 stands or stand sites from where they can hunt. Many of them have their stands in place prior to the day of the hunt, and each of these stands is in a prime deer area.

These successful outdoorsmen know how to approach these stands with a favorable wind direction. Depending on the wind direction, they eliminate the stands they can't hunt from because their scents would be carried into the hunting areas.

In Your Stand

If you are hunting from the best stand you can choose, have found the most productive place in the woods and are in your treestand at the deer's prime moving times, but then you fall asleep, daydream or become distracted, all your time and energy are wasted. Because you have scouted and found the best region to hunt, be confident you can see the deer from this stand. When you are in your treestand, look for deer, let your eyes constantly search your surroundings, work out your game plans on when and where you will take the deer if he appears and study every log, tree and bush. Also look for the tips of a deer's antlers, watch for the white swish of a tail, and notice parallel lines that are from three to four feet off the ground, which indicate the deer's back. Concentrate on hunting.

When you no longer can focus on hunting, come out of the tree and either move to a new treestand site or go home and plan to hunt another day. Some of the most effective hunters I know may stay in their treestands only two hours in the morning and two in the afternoon. If you are in your treestand sleeping you are not hunting. Also, you risk falling out of your stand and dropping your bow or your gun.

A permanent treestand like this one may be most effective when used near greenfields that are planted every season.

Treestand hunting gives you a better view of the woods, a way to get your scent up off the ground, the opportunity to sit quietly from an elevated shooting platform for a long time and is, in my opinion, one of the very best ways to take a deer. However, knowing where to put your treestand, when to hunt from it and what to do when you are in the stand may make the difference in your success or failure as a treestand hunter.

CHAPTER 8

GETTING A BUCK WITHIN RANGE
With Ronnie Groom

TO GET A SHOT, a deer must come within range. The position of the stand is important, however, deer will often walk through an area without well-established trails, or several trails may lead into a region with no way for you to determine which is the best one to set up a stand on to bag a deer. These kinds of situations occur frequently in hunting places with high deer populations. Here are some tactics I use to funnel deer into my stand.

Using The Five Trail Tactic

When the white oak tree begins to drop its acorns in the fall, deer will concentrate under this tree to feed. But when there are five trails coming into a feeding spot, how do you know on which trail to set up?

Careful scouting will reveal that of the five trails running into a feeding area, the deer are probably using only one or two. I'll pick one of the most used trails for setting up my stand -if I'm hoping to bag any deer.

Next, I must funnel the deer off the trails I'm not hunting onto the trail I am hunting. To cancel out trails, I hang a hunting coat, a shirt or a hat about eye level to a deer on the trail I'm not going to be. Deer are naturally wary. When they see that coat, they usually will funnel off the trail they plan to utilize onto the next best trail. Also, to delete the lesser used trails, I will lay a limb or some brush across those trails. Although deer can jump over the brush, they always tend to take the path of least resistance. So they generally will walk around brush and onto the trail I plan to hunt.

Something else to remember when hunting a high deer population region is to hunt the trails that are not utilized as much - rather than the

Ronnie Groom, who takes whitetail deer each year with his bow, his blackpowder gun and his rifle, also teaches these skills in hunting schools around the country. Groom hunts deer three to four months a year and stays in touch with the latest techniques through the people who come into his sporting goods store. A consummate student of the sport of hunting deer, Groom willingly shares what he has learned.

trails with a lot of sign on them - if you prefer to take a buck. I have observed that bucks generally come into a feeding area on lesser used trails rather than the same trails a bunch of does utilize. If a buck is my target, I'll be hunting over the secondary trails rather than the primary ones.

Don't forget the wind direction will cancel out some trails. If there are trails leading into a feeding spot from five different directions, the wind may

By narrowing a funnel on the less used trails you can put a buck under your stand.

carry your human scent down three of them, ruling them out. If that's the case, then you only have to turn deer off one trail.

I successfully utilized this tactic a few years ago when I discovered an old fence line running through the woods. The deer were crossing the fence line at two places - a hole in the fence and a gap in the fence. Since I wanted to make sure I had a deer to shoot at, I piled brush in the hole and set up my stand near the gap. A buck walked to where the hole was in the fence, turned and came right down to the gap, where I took him.

Another time I chose a spot to hunt that had two trails coming out of a swamp and crossing a road. I parked my vehicle on the road in front of one trail and set my stand up near the second trail. Within a couple of hours, the deer came along the trail where I was set up. So I bagged the buck.

Narrowing The Funnel

When habitat is restricted, deer will funnel through a small neck to move from one area to another. For example, if two fields are on either side of a woodlot, often where those fields corner will be a small neck of woods that looks like the end of a funnel. Here is where the deer that want to travel between woodlots will pass through rather than having to walk through the field. These places are ideal for setting up.

However, one of the common problems is that these funnels may be 75 to 100 yards wide. If the deer walks on one side of the funnel while the hunter is set up on the other side, the sportsman may not get a shot. The neck of the funnel must be narrowed further to put the deer where you can shoot him.

Many times, natural obstacles in a funnel will help you. Often there will be an edge where maybe a creek bottom divides the funnel, and the deer naturally will walk to the edge of the creek. Or a briar thicket or some type of thick cover will serve as an edge. I search for edges within funnels, which will concentrate deer into a smaller area.

I also look for downed trees. Although deer can hop over a fallen tree, they will usually walk around it. If I can find a fallen tree in a funnel area, then I set up close to the tree - assuming the deer will walk around the tree rather than going over it. If there is no edge, no downed tree or any way to funnel the deer, then I build a brush walk across one side of the funnel. The deer will begin to move around that brush obstruction and funnel under the tree where I am.

Many funnel areas may be regions where plenty of thick brush is present- not just relatively open funnel regions found in hardwoods. These types of places may be better locations to see deer. When I locate a neck

Thick cover is where you find big bucks.

of woods where the deer are funneling through, I go in prior to the season and cut a trail through the cover. The deer will begin to utilize that trail and be right where I want them to be when the season starts.

One season I was hunting in Georgia when I encountered a bottleneck that was too wide to hunt. The night before I planned to hunt this region, we had a heavy rain. The bottleneck had some low gullies and ditches in it. Right after the rain, these low places in the funnel filled with water. The standing water narrowed the neck from 100 yards down to 20 yards. The deer could have walked through the water, which was only about six to eight inches deep, but instead they moved around the water to within 20 yards of my stand.

Human Scent Can Help

As you know, human scent spooks the deer worse than anything in the forest. To be an effective hunter, you must eliminate your human scent. However, sometimes I utilize human scent to funnel deer.

You can use human odor to cancel out areas and cause deer to move into the regions you want to hunt. Using human scent to funnel deer is most effective in places of high hunter pressure, because the deer have learned that human odor represents danger. Therefore the animals will leave an area that has human odor and go to another region.

I was once hunting St. Vincent's Island in Florida, which was a heavily hunted public area. As I walked down one side of a ridge, I left a lot of human scent all the way to the top of the ridge. Then I went downwind and slipped up the other side of the ridge. When the deer reached that point where they smelled human odor, they usually crossed the ridge heading for the thickest cover available and walked to the side where I had placed my stand.

I think the best way to set up this funneling technique is to know where the thick cover is, lay down human scent on the opposite side of the ridge from the thick cover and then take a stand close to the thicket. When the deer hit that scent trail, the trail acts like a brick wall, turning the deer and funneling them to the cover.

The best way to leave this scent trail is to go in the day before the hunt and lay down the scent trail by just walking back and forth on one side of a ridge. Then set the stand up close to heavy cover and plan to be in that stand before daylight on the following morning. Deer, which usually feed at night in areas of high hunter pressure, will smell that human odor and funnel to where the hunter wants them. However, at the beginning of the season, before many hunters have been in the woods, using human odor to cancel out areas is not nearly as effective. When the deer smell human odor early in the season, they usually will blow, snort and stomp. But they won't funnel away from human scent nearly as readily as they will later in the season.

Using Hunting Pressure To Funnel Deer

If you know where most outdoorsmen hunt most of the time, then you can concentrate deer into smaller areas. If sportsmen are hunting in the big woods that run to the edge of a thicket, most of the deer will concentrate along the edge of the thicket knowing they can dart into heavy cover if they spot or smell a hunter. Or they will concentrate in the thickets realizing that many hunters won't go in the thick cover to find a deer. But I like to go into thick areas where the deer are the most concentrated and then decide how best to bag them.

If there is a four year old clearcut with head-high bushes in it, and I know that is where the deer are concentrating, then I'll move into that thicket. Usually there's at least one tree or one high point where I can set up a stand. Most hunters will avoid this region because they can't see to shoot. But that's the reason the deer are in this thick cover.

Before the season begins, I'll move into the cover with a pair of pruning shears and hedge clippers. After deciding where I will set up my treestand, I'll cut small trails like spokes leading away from that treestand for about 30 yards. My trails only may be three or four feet wide, but that is all I need to see and take a deer. When the hunting pressure builds up, I move into that thick cover and set up where I can see down my shooting lanes.

I assume that most hunters are intelligent people, and that if they find a trail leading into thick cover, they will follow it. That's why I don't cut a trail into my stand, and I don't go to my stand from the same direction every time I hunt it. If hunters can't find my stand, which is in the thick cover that they are forcing deer into, then I have the perfect place to bag a buck. Most of the time, I will take bigger deer in the thicker cover later in the season when the hunting pressure is high.

CHAPTER 9

HOW TO STALK UNDETECTED

A STALKER IS A PART of all that is around him. He moves with the ease of a warm summer's breeze that is never seen and barely felt.

Man was not the originator of stalking techniques, but merely the imitator. He observed cats as they stalked and killed their prey. He watched the fox and other predators move in close for their attacks. Because of his primitive weapons - his spear, knife and bow and arrow - early man had to learn to stalk in close if he was to harvest game and survive.

Today, hunters can utilize various methods of stalking to bag bucks. Remember not to make noise on the way to the place you're hunting, because this action has a domino effect. As you spook animals out in front of you, these animals will move out and spook the deer in the area you're planning to stalk.

One place I stalk requires crossing a creek. I have friends who hunt this same region. They utilize an aluminum boat to cross the creek-banging around and spooking everything. When they arrive at the hunting spot, they almost always are unsuccessful in taking a deer. However, I have been successful in getting deer in this region, because I wade the creek and make little or no noise while trying to get to my hunting spot.

Hunting Trails

During the rut, hunting well-defined deer trails is one of the most effective means of stalk hunting. When the bucks are in the rut, they are usually trailing the does. Many times, a buck deer will move down a trail with his nose on the ground following a doe, hoping for a mating encounter.

A buck often will move down a game trail with his nose on the ground following a doe.

By quietly stalking down the same trail the buck is on, I have had trophy whitetails walk within easy gun range of me.

A few seasons ago I was slipping down a trail when I saw a trophy 10-point weighing over 200 pounds coming toward me. The big deer had his nose on the ground and was walking at a steady pace right down the same trail where I was. I kept my scope on the animal and allowed him to continue to move toward me. I was hunting in mature hardwoods and the deer could have easily seen me. But he never looked up, and I took him.

Stalking With A Bow

A friend of mine who still makes and uses the primitive longbow, Jerry Hill, prefers to stalk and hunt from the ground instead of from a treestand because he can see game and move to it rather than waiting for the game to come toward him. Hill enjoys making the many calculations that must be made before an arrow is released. A good stalk hunter with a bow must first determine the direction the deer is feeding. By expecting the deer to continue in that direction, the hunter can decide where he needs to be to intercept the deer.

The hunter must also determine wind direction because he cannot move where the wind will take his scent to the feeding deer. He wants to

Jerry Hill uses the longbow very effectively to bag bucks.

move to the point where he can intercept the deer without alarming the animal with his scent.

A stalker must observe what type of cover is available for him to move through so the deer won't see him, what natural barriers like rivers or thickets will prevent either the hunter or the animal from arriving at their intercept point at the same time, and whether the stalk will involve circling the deer and losing eye contact with him before the hunter arrives at the point where he plans to take a shot. A stalker must make these evaluations immediately after he spots the deer and before he even starts to move.

Oftentimes, a stalker may spook a deer and that's not necessarily bad, especially with young deer. Sometimes spooking the deer may be an advantage. A young deer will run from movement he doesn't understand. But after he has been gone for awhile, he will often return to investigate that movement and try and figure out what spooked him. If you don't get a shot before you spook a deer, many times within 30 minutes to an hour, if you stay still in the same spot, the animal will walk back in for a look-see, and you can take him.

Stalking Hills

Hunting hills may be the most difficult way to stalk because vision is limited by the hills on either side. When I'm hunting hills, I assume the buck will see me first.

The most important ingredient then in my success is to know the terrain and the deer's escape routes. When you jump a buck between two hills, he may run straight away for a distance. But unless he has picked up your scent, he generally will circle to either the right or the left and come back to see what has spooked him.

I begin my stalk between two hills, starting at the base of a valley, and walking the little gullies or streams that come down between the two ridges. Often, I will hear the deer get up. However, even if I don't, I assume I have spooked the deer. When I reach the top of the hill, I turn around and walk right back down between the same two hills I've just walked up. Then when I get to the base, I move over to the next hollow, either to the right or the left. If I know the deer's escape route, I know which hollow to go up. But if I'm not sure, I have a 50 percent chance of seeing him whether I go right or left.

As I start up the second hollow, I move very slowly and quietly. I prefer to stalk in boots with soles that are almost worn out so I can feel twigs and sticks under my feet and attempt not to break them. If I've guessed right, I'll catch the deer moving on the opposite side of the hill that I just have stalked up. Generally a buck will circle and go back to the hollow where he has been frightened. What I try to do is intercept him on his return route.

Slipping Down Roads

One of the disadvantages of stalk hunting is you can't help making some noise while moving through the woods. That's why I prefer to stalk

By planning your stalk, you may be able to get in very close to a buck before he spots you.

down logging roads, hiking trails, firebreaks or any manmade path through the woods. Fewer leaves and sticks will be on these paths, and a hunter can move more quietly than through the woods.

The exception is when the road or the path goes through a vast expanse of open cover where the hunter will be silhouetted against a skyline on a ridgetop or where the road may meander through a clearcut, and a deer can see the hunter coming from a half mile away. Most of the time if a hunter

By wearing chest-high waders you can stalk through water silently and without leaving your scent.

walks slowly, no more than one mile for every 2-1/2- hours spent in the woods, he will see and take deer from the road. The only technique I've found more productive for me than road slipping is water stalking.

Stalking The Water

I discovered this method of stalk hunting a few years ago when the river bottom swamp I hunted became flooded. Then the only access available to some of the best hunting territory was through a thigh-high slough. However, instead of wading through the slough and coming out on the bank on the other side, I used a pair of waders to stay in the slough and stalk.

I prefer to wear lightweight waders with a small innertube float at the top of the waders, which is extremely helpful when -not if - I step into a stump hole. However, they are not designed for woods hunting -especially wading through places that may have briars and thorns. For this reason, I put on a pair of canvas hunting britches over my waders. Then I can wade through the flooded sloughs and underwater briars and not puncture the waders.

Moving through the water offers several advantages that land hunters do not have. Deer are not expecting a hunter to be in the water. Water provides a natural barrier between man and deer. When an expanse of water is between a deer and hunting pressure, the animal feels more secure and moves more freely.

I make very little noise, if any, as I move through the water. I try and move slowly enough so that no waves or ringlets are noticeable on the water's surface to spook the deer. Too, I leave no scent on the ground I travel because it is all underwater. I spook very little game as I stalk. I have had beavers, muskrats and wood ducks swim within 10 to 15 yards of where I'm standing, never see me and never be spooked.

Usually my water stalking is in flooded timber. If I see a deer off in the distance, I almost always can keep a tree between the buck and myself while I am stalking closer for a shot. Even if the deer spots me in the water, he rarely will spook, because he is accustomed to seeing animals in the water. Nothing in the water ever has indicated danger to him. The water and the standing timber breaks up my form. Therefore, the deer doesn't see the outline of a man when he looks at me - at least not most of the time.

In a freshly flooded woodlot, many of the acorns and other foods deer thrive on float to the surface and ring the edge of the water - like a bathtub ring. Deer will move along the edges of the slough to feed on this food. Most of the time I will see several deer in one morning when stalking in the water. Oftentimes the deer will be out in the slough with me - feeding or swimming from one bank to the other.

I never have spooked a swimming deer. When the animal comes out of the water, he usually will hesitate for a minute and present a good shot instead of running off as soon as he's on land.

CHAPTER 10

HOW TO CALL DEER
With Dr. Larry Marchinton

IF YOU'VE BEEN WONDERING what a hunter is saying to a deer when he blows a call and which calls are the most effective at luring in deer, our research team at the University of Georgia has identified 13 different sounds (only one is non-vocal - the foot stomp) whitetail deer make.

We have defined deer vocalization as sounds deer make to communicate with one another. But we're just in the infant stages of learning how deer communicate. At this point, we're trying to learn what questions to ask about deer communications rather than coming up with some hard-formed conclusions. Although deer may very well have a language, we don't know this for sure. Remember deer vocalization is a relatively new area of investigation.

The first papers containing scientific data on deer vocalization were published in 1981 - one at the University of Michigan by a gentleman named Richardson and the other at about the same time by Tom Atkinson for his PhD dissertation at the University of Georgia.

From these two papers and the resulting ongoing research, biologists now know that deer do communicate a lot of information through the sounds they make, including alarm, aggression, the desire to mate and the wish to make contact, as well as calls between the mothers and fawns and many more calls that we don't know about at this time.

Distress Calls
Two calls indicate distress - the snort and the bawl. Most hunters have heard the snort, which is an alarm call deer use. I personally believe the

Dr. Larry Marchinton has been a deer behavioral scientist for many years at the University of Georgia. Through radio telemetry and careful observations, Marchinton and his staff have added a wealth of scientific information to our knowledge of deer. When a hunter wants to know why a deer does what it does, Marchinton is one of the men most often quoted.

snort communicates that there's danger in the area. Some research tends to indicate that when a deer snorts, he's trying to solicit some type of response from the animal or person at which he's snorting. When a deer snorts, he senses danger, which may mean he's using this type of communication to make a predator show itself.

A graduate student at the University of Georgia utilized the snort to call in deer. If the snort was strictly an alarm call, then the snort wouldn't have been able to lure deer.

The bawl, which is a cry of pain, can be made on a modified predator call. The bawl is effective for the hunter to call up does. Occasionally I've seen a buck come to the bawl, but this call apparently stimulates the maternal response of the deer. Although the bawl seems to be most productive right after fawning season, deer will come to this call even later on in the fall.

Antagonistic Or Aggressive Sounds

Basically three antagonistic or aggressive sounds are given by the mature buck - the grunt, the grunt/snort and the grunt/snort/wheeze. The grunt is a low guttural sound utilized by both sexes throughout the year. It is the lowest intensity of antagonistic interaction.

The grunt/snort is a more intense call than the grunt made by both sexes. This call is given by making a grunt sound and immediately following the grunt with rapid snorts. This is not the same type of snort that's an alarm call and is long and drawn out. The snorts that follow a grunt are short and choppy. When a deer gives this call, he's making a more serious threat to the deer and the animals to which he's talking.

The grunt/snort/wheeze, the most aggressive call a deer vocalizes, is made with a grunt followed by one to four snorts and then a wheeze. When a deer gives this call, he's telling another deer or the animals that are threatening him that he's serious, and something is going to happen.

Mating Calls

The grunt call used most often by the hunter does not fall in the category of aggressive calls but comes under the heading of tending or mating calls. The tending grunt is more drawn out, and the sound of the grunt actually lasts longer than the aggressive grunt. The aggressive grunt is shorter and more choppy than the tending grunt. The tending grunt is the call the deer voices when he's tending a doe. But even if the hunters get these two calls confused, the grunt still may have the same effect of drawing in a buck, because he may come to the call either to fight or to mate.

The grunt call, whether it is a tending grunt or an aggressive grunt, can run off a subordinate buck. The aggressive grunt almost always will scare off a subordinate buck. However, the tending grunt may draw in a subordinate buck that hopes he may be able to breed the doe that's with the other buck.

The phlegm and sniff is a kind of squeaky noise the deer makes when he curls his lip up. This call usually is given by a buck when he first smells estrous urine. Oftentimes bucks will give this call whether the urine is estrous or not.

The Contact Call

The contact call is given primarily by does and fawns of both sexes. This too is a type of grunt. But this contact call is longer and not quite as low as the other grunts, and is somewhat higher pitched because it's made by the does and fawns. The contact call seems to tell other deer, "I'm over here. Come find me." Quite often I've heard this call given by fawns separated from their does.

We've learned that the grunt call in its various levels of intensity and different tones is used by deer to communicate many things at different times, which is perhaps one of the reasons that commercial grunt calls often tend to be so effective. Even if you give the wrong grunt call, you still may lure in the deer.

For instance, if you mean to give a tending grunt, but you don't know the difference between a tending grunt and an aggressive grunt, and the sound you give communicates aggression, you still may call in a deer. Instead of calling in a buck that may want to mate, you may call in a buck that prefers to fight, which is what makes deer calling so different from other types of animal calling. If you give the wrong call when you're duck or turkey calling, more than likely you'll spook the game - but not when calling deer.

Fawn Calls

The mew is a high-pitched call that's not as loud as the bleat. The mew seems to be a call that the doe utilizes to keep from getting lost or just to be recognized.

The bleat is louder and longer than the mew, and much more intense. Fawns often will use the bleat when they want to feed. The bleat is quite similar to a contact call and is often used by the hunter to say to the deer, "Hello, I'm over here. Come find me."

The nursing whine is a sound fawns vocalize when they're nursing or when they want to nurse.

Techniques For Calling Deer

Hunters now are beginning to understand and effectively use deer calls. Whether we'll ever reach the level of communication a duck hunter

When a buck curls his lips up and sniffs, he most often has smelled estrous urine.

has when he calls in a flight of ducks is still speculative. Deer have bigger brains than ducks and are not fooled quite as easily.

Besides being a deer researcher, I'm also an avid deer hunter. Occasionally I play with all the calls to see what kind of results I'll get. But the call I utilize most is the tending grunt. I use my mouth to call deer most of the time rather than commercial calls.

I also use deer calls in conjunction with rattling. A call that I feel can be very effective is what I have named the straining grunt. Hunters

A grunt call often increases a hunter's odds for taking a buck.

acquainted with the rattling technique of hunting deer understand that clashing the antlers simulates two bucks fighting. From observing bucks fighting, I know they give off a grunting sound similar to that made by two linemen when they try to push and shove each other out of the way to make a hole for the running back. So I call this grunt the straining grunt, which is a deep guttural sound that's somewhere between a roar and a grunt. Although on several occasions I've called deer using this call, I'm sure at other times I've run deer off with it. The key to utilizing this grunt successfully is to put a strained sound in the call. But a hunter must realize this call may scare off any buck except the most dominant in the area.

Calling deer as a hunting tactic is so new, and scientists are learning so much about calling, that we're just now able to ask better questions to find out what we don't understand. However, biologists do know that deer

Some buck fights are simply sparring matches to establish dominance.

calling is not a sure fire way to always bring in bucks. But since calling is productive, I sometimes use it when hunting.

The key to successful deer calling is to use the correct calls at the right times of the year. For instance, the most effective time to use the tending grunt is during breeding season. In the early part of hunting season if you want to call in a doe, then common sense tells you to use some fawn-in-distress calls or contact calls. If you're hunting in an area where the buck and doe ratio is so out of balance that not many bucks are present, and you want to harvest a doe, then rattle. In regions with few bucks and large numbers of does, the does will respond to anything that sounds like a buck, especially in the latter part of the season.

However, calling in a buck is extremely difficult when there are many more does than bucks. I don't know if we've identified a call that can be considered effective to call in a buck when few are in an area.

Where there is a more balanced buck/doe ratio and some older bucks are in the herd, you can use the tending grunt - especially after most of the does have been bred - to call in a buck. Rattling is also effective to call in a buck in a region with a balanced buck/doe ratio.

Antler rattling, which is a form of deer communication, falls into two categories - sparring matches and buck fights. Sparring matches are not true fights and usually take place early in the season right after the velvet is shed from the buck's antlers. During this testing time, each buck learns his position in the herd and is placed in the pecking order. As the season progresses, and the does go into the rut, full-blown fights take place. The fights happen when two dominant bucks or two that think they're dominant, come into conflict over a doe.

Once you understand the difference in the two types of deer fights, you have to adapt the severity of your rattling techniques to the time of the year you're hunting. If you're hunting early in deer season when the bucks are forming their pecking order, then tinkling the antlers - just lightly hitting the tips together - is best. If you're rattling during the rut, you need to clash the antlers together with a lot of force and grunt to simulate a full-blown fight.

But once again, rattling antlers is not a sure fire way to bring in a dominant buck. I've seen dominant bucks that have been tending does actually veer away from fights. Researchers believe they move away from a fight to keep from losing the does they're tending.

Although information about deer vocalization and deer calling will make you more knowledgeable about the deer you hunt, remember deer calling is not a magic cure. Calling deer doesn't replace the importance of the hunter's knowledge of the animal or the hunter's woodsmanship. The ability to call deer is just another aid that on certain days under specific conditions may bring a buck in to where the hunter is.

CHAPTER 11

USING MAN DRIVES EFFECTIVELY
With Don Taylor

AN EFFECTIVE MAN DRIVE often takes far fewer people than most hunters assume. Two men can drive deer aswell as 20 men can. But the hunters must understand each other's hunting methods a well as the deer's movement patterns.

Mountain Driving

Sportsmen who hunt hills and mountains must be as familiar with the bottoms and the sides of the mountains where the deer like to bed as the deer are. One tactic that works for mountain drivers is getting together before daylight on the day of the hunt and deciding which ridges and hollows they will drive. Driving is probably not the correct term to use, since slipping probably better describes what they do.

To move the deer, one of the mountain drivers slips from the bottom of two hills up a draw to the top of a hill. The other hunter will stand silently at the top of the hill. The hunter who is slipping through the woods oftentimes will get a shot at the deer. But more than likely he will cause the deer to move up the draw toward the standing hunter.

Instead of running from the driver, the deer will usually be slipping and looking back at the hunter walking up the draw. Some hunters on a two-man drive make a mistake by having the driver make noise to spook the deer. If he does spook the deer and drive the animal past the other hunter, many times the deer will be running rather than walking, presenting a much harder shot. Using the technique of slip driving, sometimes you can slip up on a deer, shoot him and take him before he moves up the ridge.

Don Taylor often spooks deer out of their beds and still gets off a shot.

When two men are driving together, one slipping and the other standing, knowing when the one who is slipping will begin to drive toward the stander is very important. For instance, when a deer is close to the top of a ridge, as soon as he smells, sees or hears the hunter who is slipping, the deer will start moving out of his bedding area. The stander may bag the buck within 10 minutes of when the other hunter has started slipping.

Successful two-man driving in the hills must involve several ingredients. First you have to have an idea of where the deer are. Next you have to know the escape routes the deer most often use to leave a bottom or a hollow. Finally, you've got to realize exactly when the hunter will begin moving and make sure both of you have on hunter orange.

Single Man Driving

Don Taylor's favorite tactic is utilizing a single man drive. Many things in the woods spook deer momentarily, but just because a deer is spooked does not mean he is terrified. A spooked deer is much like a man who has someone jump out from behind a tree and shout, "Boo!" He may be startled for a moment, and he may run five or six yards before he realizes nothing really has happened to frighten him.

Oftentimes, Taylor hunts into the wind, quietly and slowly. Many times he will spook deer out of their beds. Sometimes these deer will run off 20 or 30 yards. Then they will stop and look back over their shoulders. If they don't see him, they may put their heads down and begin to feed. Several times Taylor has used this single man drive tactic to roust bucks out of their beds, drive them into the open and then take a shot when they've stopped to look back.

If the deer is unable to pick up human scent and if the hunter remains motionless after spooking him, then the deer usually won't leave the immediate vicinity. But if the deer ever picks up the hunter's scent or sees him move, he will be gone.

Thick Cover/Driving

Some bucks are never taken from the woods because hunters never put enough pressure to move them out of their daytime haunts. Some areas are absolutely prohibitive to the hunter, such as thickets, clearcuts or briar patches. Once you realize the deer's sanctuary is in these hard-to-reach places, then the hunter who braves the briars and the bushes can move the deer out of their haunts. However, you must understand that if a deer gets up in thick cover you will have little, if any, chance of taking him.

Driving thick cover can be the key to taking big bucks.

Here's the hunter's dilemma. The outdoorsman knows the deer are in thick cover. The deer realizes that the sportsman will not penetrate that cover. If the hunter does go in to take the deer, the deer can escape unseen. This is the perfect condition for a man drive.

Oftentimes from five to 20 men may be required to walk deer out of a thicket. The hunters may not be more than 20 yards apart as they plow through the brush. But many times the standers on the edge of the thicket will get open, clear shots - usually running shots - at the deer as they break free from the cover. A well-organized man drive in thick cover can produce some of the biggest and best bucks on any piece of property if the thick cover has been driven only rarely during the season.

For four or five years in a row, a certain small group of hunters brought in six to eight trophy bucks each season to my taxidermy business. Sometimes the same hunter would bring in two or three trophies and have them mounted.

Finally one day when curiosity gave way to indiscretion, I asked them to tell me how they were hunting to take this many bucks. They informed me they made many short drives in a day - often as many as 10 to 15. They never drove over 10 acres of property at a time. Usually the drives were only 15 to 20 minutes long. They looked for small heads of woods or briar patches close to main roads or main arteries in the woods. They searched for spots no one would want to hunt, like drainage ditches in the middle of a field, a big blackberry thicket next to an old logging road or some other kind of very thick cover close to well-traveled roads. Then they used the roads to get to these briarpatches quickly and easily.

One or two men went into the cover while the other men took stands on the edge of the cover. If a deer was in that small scope of woods and briars, they usually could drive him out in five to 10 minutes. When the deer came out of the cover, often the standers would get a shot. If no deer fled from the briar patch, then the hunters loaded up quickly, moved to another head of woods and put on another short hunt without wasting any time.

Elements Of A Good Man Drive

Several elements must come together to make up a productive man drive. The hunters need to ...

... Know where the deer are or which direction or trails the deer probably will use to escape from an area. Then standers can be set up where they will do the most good.

... Let the number of standers and drivers available determine the size of the region they drive. Too few drivers on a large expanse of land will make an ineffective mandrive.

... Invade several small heads of woods in a short time with a small group of hunters who know where to hunt to take advantage of covering the most ground.

CHAPTER 12

WHEN DEER BECOME NOCTURNAL
With Ronnie Groom

I BELIEVE THE TERM nocturnal is inappropriate when referring to deer. The deer may not feed or move during daylight hours where the sportsmen are in the woods, but the deer are feeding and moving somewhere. Deer never stay in their beds for 12 to 15 hours at a time. They get up, they move around, and they eat. But they don't conduct these activities during daylight hours where there's heavy hunter pressure.

However, after dark, the deer may travel into the regions where hunters have been. When the outdoorsman sees deer tracks and signs of feeding and/or rubbing, and he realizes deer are utilizing this area only at night, he deduces the deer have become nocturnal. Actually the deer are nocturnal only because that's when they use the land where the hunter is during the day. Hunters cause deer to be nocturnal in a region by wandering through the forests leaving human scent all over the ground to spook deer.

To find a spot where the deer are moving in the daytime, you must search for a deer sanctuary. However, most of the time when a hunter locates a site like this, he will run the deer out of the sanctuary with his human scent. Then he won't be able to hunt this particular place until the next season.

How To Find A Deer Sanctuary

I use aerial photos of the property I'm hunting to locate big buck sanctuaries. There probably aren't a great deal of signs leading to or away from these hideouts. When hunting pressure is high, the dumb bucks die

Big bucks often will feed and move only after dark, particularly when hunting pressure is high.

early in the season. Only the older, smarter bucks have learned to feed at night in open places and hole up in the daytime in sanctuaries. You may not see very many, if any, deer. More than likely you're hunting two or three bucks, at the most, in a sanctuary.

Sanctuaries generally occur in spots with no hunting pressure. A sanctuary can be a small island in the middle of a woods pond, a small patch of grass or weeds in a field, a briar thicket right behind a farmhouse or a big thicket 1-1/2-miles away from the closest hunter and far from the traveled roads.

Hunters cause deer to be nocturnal. Therefore, deer will move during daylight hours where the hunters aren't. The problem with hunting these secret places is that if you go in, travel around in them and then try and hunt in these regions, you'll spook the deer. The bucks will move to another place. To take bucks when they're nocturnal, first discover where they're holding during the daytime. Then hunt these regions very little.

How To Hunt A Deer Sanctuary

Once you discover a deer sanctuary, more than likely you shouldn't hunt it that same season. If you go into the area, you will run the deer out of it. But I mark the sanctuaries I discover on a map. Then I can return to them prior to the beginning of the next hunting season - when the whitetails aren't using the sanctuaries - and lay out a game plan. I decide which way I can approach the sanctuary and how I can travel in the region. Then I pick out a stand site. If it is an area with heavy cover, I go ahead and cut shooting lanes so I can see to take a buck.

I consult my compass to know what wind direction I must have to approach the sanctuary without having my scent carried into the hunting zone. I usually will prepare eight to 10 sanctuaries to be hunted when the time is right -when the deer become nocturnal. Then I leave these places alone and don't return until I'm prepared to take a buck.

Knowing when to hunt the deer sanctuaries is the most critical ingredient for bagging nocturnal bucks. I may have only one or two days during hunting season to hunt the sanctuaries I have prepared. But I will never go to one of these hideouts until all the conditions are right. I never hunt these spots during the beginning of hunting season. I'm allowing hunting pressure to work for me, rather than against me, by letting it build up in the regions around my sanctuaries. Therefore I wait until near the end of the season before I try to hunt these sanctuaries.

When the deer become nocturnal, they will move during daylight hours in the sanctuaries. Late in the season when hunting pressure is intense and the wind is right, I slip into the area before daylight and wait for a buck to appear. Once I hunt a sanctuary, I won't return to that same spot for at least a week or two. I realize that if I hunt this site too much, then I will run the deer out and won't have a chance to harvest the bucks. That's why I develop several stands before the season. Then I have a couple of places to hunt with the wind coming from different wind directions.

Hunt The Food

Deer first become nocturnal, particularly in feeding regions, because so many hunters try to bag deer as the animals come in to feed. Therefore the deer know better than to move into these types of sites during daylight hours.

115

Knowing what a deer sanctuary is and when to hunt it is often the key to taking a trophy like this.

However, the deer also understand that when darkness approaches, the hunters leave the woods. Although the animals won't move into the feeding sites until dark, they generally will start toward these feeding regions before dark. If the hunter follows the trails that lead from the feeding area to the bedding region or the places where the bucks are seeking sanctuary, he can take a stand close to this thick cover.

Most people make two mistakes when they're hunting nocturnal deer in the vicinity of their feeding regions. They often leave their stands too early to bag a deer, fearing that they're going to get lost in the woods after dark. When a hunter moves out of the forests when enough light is still available, they are leaving before the deer show up, even though they may have their stands in the best place possible.

To bag a buck like this you may have to let quite a few small bucks pass by you.

Successful hunters remain in their stands until the light is too little to see to shoot. Most of the time, a buck will not appear until the last five to 10 minutes of daylight. He realizes that by the time he reaches the feeding area, the woods will be too dark for the hunters. Then he can feed undisturbed. The hunter who harvests this deer will have to remain in his stand until black dark if he is going to see the buck.

The hunters' second mistake when hunting nocturnal deer in their feeding areas is shooting the first bucks they see. To take a really nice buck, you must allow the small bucks to pass by. Remember that the big bucks haven't grown large by being stupid. They will let the smaller, less experienced bucks walk out into an opening first. Big bucks assume that if a hunter is out there the little bucks will die first. To take a truly large deer as he is moving from a thicket, a sanctuary or a bedding area, most of the time you must let the small deer pass by you, undisturbed.

Hunting Nocturnal Bucks In The Morning

Large bucks will travel from their feeding regions to some type of cover early in the morning. The deer have learned that most sportsmen will hunt until about 9:00 or 10:00 A.M. before giving up and heading back to their vehicles. They also realize that hunters don't hunt in the middle of the day. So this is when big bucks will move to take advantage of the deer hunter's predictable movement patterns.

To hunt bucks when they are nocturnal, I come to my stand well before daylight and catch the deer traveling in sparse cover on their way to deep cover. In high pressure areas, I've learned to stay in my stand when other hunters aren't hunting. In addition to few sportsmen being in their stands before daylight, there are few hunters in their stands between 11:00 A.M. and 2:00 P.M. These are the times to hunt bucks that have been branded as nocturnal.

Deer that are moving in the middle of the day and don't want to go into the thickets will feed along the edges of thickets where plenty of food may be available. A big buck may travel along that edge and begin to feed in the middle of the day for two reasons. He knows food is there, and, secondly, he realizes that if danger does approach, he's within two steps of cover. He also understands that the hunters are not moving during the middle of the day. Therefore, the likelihood of a hunter encounter is extremely slim.

Nocturnal Deer Tactics

There are certain hunting techniques that the sportsmen who want to take these phantom deer must employ. Being conscious of the wind direction is the most critical ingredient to taking a nocturnal buck. This rule absolutely cannot be broken. Don't hunt a region where you believe a phantom buck is hiding if the wind is not in your face.

Another factor that most sportsmen don't consider when they're hunting nocturnal bucks is when the hunt actually begins. Hunting nocturnal deer involves attempting to bag one of the smartest deer in all of the woods. Since this buck has learned how to dodge the hunters in the woods, he is much smarter than the bucks that die early in the season. To harvest this kind of buck, you must start to hunt when you leave your vehicle and enter the woods. You can't slam doors, cough, spit or talk. You must be as quiet as if you think the buck is watching you the entire time.

Approach your hunting site slowly and deliberately. In preparing to hunt this particular deer, besides already pre-determining your stand site,

Taking the buck is the fulfillment of the sport of deer hunting.

you should know the route you're going to take to that stand. Clear out the brush along that path ahead of time. Then when you stalk to the stand, your clothes won't brush up against the foliage and make noise. Be sure to wear soft clothing so you can move silently. Allow yourself 30 more minutes than what you estimate you'll need to reach the stand. Then you can approach the stand slowly, quietly and deliberately with plenty of time to spare.

Leaves and limbs at your stand site should also be cleared away ahead of time. Then when you sit on the ground, you won't make any noise. If you're going to use a treestand, either put it up early in the season or know that you'll be able to set it up silently.

Once you climb into your stand before daylight, hunt with your ears before you hunt with your eyes. Many times if the deer are feeding on acorns, you can hear them popping the nuts before you can see them. If they are traveling through water, you can hear them sloshing. Or, if they are walking through leaves, you can hear them move too. You will often be able to pinpoint exactly where the deer are before you even have enough light to shoot.

Once you bag your buck and fill your tag for the season, the hunt for the next year's buck starts. Go back into the woods without a gun during hunting season when the hunting pressure is high and locate areas that the nocturnal bucks are utilizing. Many times you will run the bucks out of their sanctuaries as you move in to look for them. But since you've already filled your tag, whether or not you spook the bucks doesn't really matter.

Most hunters stop hunting when they fill their tags, therefore, they learn very little about what the deer continue doing when the hunting pressure is high. But if you begin your hunting preparation for next season after you've completed your hunt for this season, you'll be much more likely to find and take big bucks next year.

Prior to the opening of the season, move into the sanctuary areas located at the end of last year's hunting season, set up stand sites, cut shooting lanes and prepare for a successful hunting season. Then when hunting season arrives, the hunting pressure is high, and the bucks become nocturnal, just wait for them.

CHAPTER 13

LEGENDARY DEER AND THE MEN
WHO HUNT THEM

OLD SCARFACE WAS the ugliest deer that ever had come through my taxidermy shop. The animal was a mass of jagged scars, scrapes and head wounds. Usually when a deer was badly scarred, we would cut the scars out and resew the hide. But so many places on this deer were missing hair that this procedure was not possible.

When I told the out-of-state hunter on the phone I wouldn't be able to repair all the bad markings on the deer, he said, "I don't want the scars removed. That deer is Old Scarface. He has outsmarted every hunter on our club for over six years. He has been shot at, missed, hit, seen and driven every hunter on the club crazy.

"For awhile, we almost believed he was a ghost, because no gun could bring him down. We tried driving, stalking, standing and every other tactic known to man to bag that deer. But until I finally took him, nothing worked. That deer was a warrior, a credit to his breed and a legend in our part of the country."

Old Scarface is but one of the legendary deer to come through my taxidermy shop in the last 20-years.

Characteristics Of A Legend

The best deer hunters in America today hunt legends. These men have taken enough deer in their lifetimes to prove their prowess. Bagging a deer, any deer, is no longer a feat for these veteran woodsmen. Instead they enjoy

121

A trophy buck like this one taken by John Moss is usually a legend anywhere you hunt him.

pitting their woods skills against the best of the breed - the legendary mossy horns - that are few and far between.

As one of these sportsmen said recently, "Finding a real deer to hunt is getting harder and harder."

When this man specified a "real deer," he did not mean just any deer. He was talking about a deer that ...

     ... might require several seasons to take,

     ... was at least three years old. Most of the time the animal would be five years old or older to be considered a real deer,

     ... had survived many hunter encounters,

... fed almost exclusively at night which made taking him that much more difficult,

... had a bedding area in thick cover or in cover where he could spot a hunter approaching from a great distance,

... knew the routine of most of the hunters who tried to take him,

... did not throw caution to the wind during the rut,

... utilized does and younger bucks as sentinels when he traveled,

... moved only through thick cover if he moved in daylight hours,

... had habits, haunts and peculiarities which had to be learned before taking a shot could be considered,

... was believed to be smarter than man,

... had been shot at and educated by a great many hunters over a long period of time,

... was thought to be untakable and

... was a legend.

This legendary deer is the best of his breed. If not taken, he probably will die of natural causes in one or two more years. He has the personality of a fox, the cunning of a cat, the speed of a cheetah, the illusiveness of a chameleon and the nature of a ghost. These legends are the challenges for the true trophy hunter. The weight of the deer and the size of his antlers are not nearly as important as the reputation the animal has obtained.

Researching A Legend

To bag a deer with the characteristics of a legend, most veteran hunters start their research not in the woods but on the front porch of a clubhouse or around the pot-bellied stove of the local general store, close to where the legend roams.

By interviewing the outdoorsmen who have hunted the legend, the experienced hunter gathers much needed information. The interviews will reveal where the deer goes, how he acts, where he has been shot at, where he likes to bed, what he looks like, which tactics have been tried, what the legend does before, during and after the rut and 101 other characteristics.

From listening to all the stories, the veteran hunter can begin to understand the deer's personality. He also will know what techniques will not or have not worked. He will learn the region where the animal has had a lead encounter and is not likely to show up again. He will begin to understand as much about the men who hunt the legend as the animal knows about them.

Utilizing all his experience from years of hunting, the veteran now will begin to discard tactics and areas to hunt that he feels will not allow him a shot at the legend. Most novice legend hunters fail because they do not get the facts before entering the woods. One or two days spent gathering information from other hunters can save weeks or years of hunting in the woods.

Going In After Him

One of the tactics that has produced legends is what I call going in after the deer. Since a trophy deer only will travel in thick cover during daylight hours, most of his moving time may be just at dawn and at dusk. Once you know the thick cover a legend uses to travel through to get to food, water or his bed, then you have a chance to bag your trophy.

However, a common mistake made by novice legend hunters is to sit on the edge of cover and hope to take a quick shot as the buck enters or leaves the thick places. Since a trophy buck knows he is the most vulnerable on the edge of the thicket, all of his senses will be keenly tuned. He will look, smell and listen for danger. He will spend a lot of time hunting the hunter.

If the deer finds the hunter, he may retreat back into the thicket or choose another route out. If he does not sense the hunter, he often still will move quickly and quietly and use whatever cover remains to cross a sparsely vegetated area- giving the sportsman perhaps only a glimpse of the deer.

The woods-wise hunter will take a different approach to the deer. Instead of waiting for the deer to come out of the thicket, the veteran will go into the thicket with the deer. In a thick place will be trails where the animal travels. Often the trophy hunter only may have five to 15-yards field of view. He may have to sit in briars or in a cramped position for many hours or for days. But he realizes the deer feels comfortable in the thicket. Therefore the trophy will not be as wary in a thicket as he will be on the edge of a thicket. The animal will move slowly through the cover and present a better target.

Although the outdoorsman knows his chances are at least 50 to 60 percent better in the thicket than on the outer edge of the cover, he still will employ a scent disguise and camouflage and sit as motionless as possible for as long as is required to kill the legend. To take a legend in thick cover is a very strenuous ordeal. Patience and physical stamina are mandatory. Probably 90 percent of the hunters in this country cannot outlast a big buck in thick cover. However, the men who do are the true trophy hunters. They take the legends because they pay the price to go after them.

A buck of this size will be a legend in most areas where he's found.

Overnighting For Bucks

A legendary deer only may move during the first few minutes of daylight or just at dusk. When he does travel from one place to another, he may be well away from a road or an easy access area. So night navigation may be required of the hunter for him to get into position to take a shot. Although the novice trophy hunter may know how to use a compass, he may be reluctant to stake his life on his compass reading ability for a three or four mile hike before daylight or after dark to take a trophy. But the legend hunter is an excellent woods navigator by day or by night. He will enter an area. Then after finding where the buck travels early and late, he will plan to stay at the place until he takes the legend.

The seasoned woodsman expects to spend one to three days kneeling on the ground well away from other hunters. He anticipates eating cold food and spending the night without a campfire. He knows that if he does down the legend, he may have to wait until the next day to get the deer out. So he is prepared to field dress the deer. He is in shape for a long, hard drag the next morning. Spending the night in the woods may include his being rained on or snowed on, but the veteran is prepared for whatever weather conditions are dealt him.

The trophy deer hunter realizes that to take a legend, he must pay a higher price. Lesser men will pay a lesser price for failure. For the legend, the hunter must equal the hunted in experience and cunning.

Tree Sitting

Contrary to what some hunters may think, often legendary deer live on public lands with high hunter pressure. These deer understand the average hunter very well. They know most outdoorsmen will walk across two ridges or about 1/4- to 1/2-mile away from their vehicles early in the morning. These hunters will sit in the same spots for about two hours.

Then deciding they are not in the right regions, they will move to other locations and sit for about two hours more. Around 11:00 A.M., they will head back to their trucks to meet their friends for lunch. At 1:00 P.M. these same hunters will go back into the woods and sit at two different locations during the afternoon until 45 minutes before dark and then head for their trucks again.

These are the usual hunting tactics of most public land hunters. Some will bag deer. A few may take trophies. But none probably will bag a legend.

A legend hunter must have endurance. Usually most successful tree sitters have an abundance of this quality. The tree sitter understands what the legendary deer knows. Both the hunter and the hunted have learned the people pattern of heavily hunted woods.

The legend will remain in thick cover all day long. He may move only when the hunters are gone. A veteran tree sitter will place his treestand in the thickest area he can find. He will look for a big thicket with a small opening in the middle of it where he only may be able to see five to 10 yards of fairly open ground. He will get to his tree one hour before daylight and begin his vigil. Sitting in the tree, he will watch the hole in the thick cover

Tree sitters may spend hundreds of hours in their stands each season.

from daylight until black dark. The tree sitter will not leave his stand until dark.

The tree sitters I have known have told me the best time to take a legend is just at daylight when most hunters are coming in to the woods, or between 11:00 A.M. - 1:00 P.M. when hunters are leaving for lunch or the last 45 minutes before black dark when the average hunter is headed home.

The legends will stay in the thick cover in the daylight hours. During deer season, they have learned what to expect in the daytime if they leave the cover. The only way I know to take a buck like this is to stay in a treestand all day until the animal moves. But the advantage to this type of hunting is that most often I will get a shot at the deer while he is either standing still or walking slow. I never have competition from other hunters.

The toughest thing for me to deal with is the urge to move to another place. Once I decide a legend is in a thick place, I'll stay in my treestand from before daylight until after dark as many days as necessary to take him.

Hunting legends is hard work. The men who take the super trophies are a rare, hardy breed. Although they pay the price, sometimes they still will fail to outfox the deer that have built up these reputations, even with all the knowledge the legend hunters have.

For the legend hunters, the contest is the prize. Taking the legend is an added bonus. Legends are an unusual breed of deer, and to bag them often requires a unique breed of hunter.

CHAPTER 14

HOW TO HUNT THE RUT
With Dr. Karl Miller and Bob Zaiglin

IF YOU UNDERSTAND what causes the rut, when the rut occurs and what bucks do during the rut, you can increase your odds for bagging a mature whitetail each season. There are as many myths about the whitetail's mating season as there are proven scientific facts. To determine what the rut means to the deer hunter and how to hunt the rut more effectively, it is wise to ask wildlife scientists.

Trophy Bucks
Big bucks are not hard to take, according to Dr. Karl Miller.
If you're in a place where big deer are, then bagging a trophy buck is not that difficult. If not, finding a place to hunt where big deer live can be a difficult task.

In many states with large deer populations and large numbers of hunters, the highest percentage of animals taken are 1-1/2-year old bucks. The next largest percentage are the 2-1/2-year old bucks, with the older age class deer representing the smallest number of deer harvested each season. Finding a place where there's a trophy buck to hunt usually is more of a problem than actually hunting a trophy buck.

To become a trophy, a buck must be at least 3-1/2- years old, since deer usually reach their prime in the 3-1/2- to 5-1/2-year old age classes. Before you even can begin to discuss taking a trophy buck, you must first locate a region where a trophy buck lives.

Dr. Karl Miller has been studying deer since the first day he went hunting for them. His passion for the sport has led to his studies and the completion of his PhD in wildlife science. Each year, Miller and other wildlife scientists working with him at the University of Georgia's Forest Resources Department learn more about the whitetail deer, his physiology, his behavior and his habits.

The best place to take a trophy buck is in the areas where you find the fewest hunters. A big buck will leave plenty of sign by marking his territory, making scrapes and rubs and leaving a big footprint. A trophy deer wants to announce to his world that he's the dominant buck and is exerting his dominance throughout his realm.

The hunter should be able to read and understand the signs of the dominant one, just like the other bucks in the area do. During the rut, the trophy buck is going to make scrapes and freshen up those scrapes in hopes of attracting a doe he can breed. If he's not bothered with a lot of hunting

The trophy buck will make rubs to let other deer know that he is there.

pressure, he'll check these scrapes during daylight hours in the time of the rut. Therefore, if you can find a trophy buck in a remote region that few, if any, hunters are going into, then you can take him - if you know how to read his signs and locate his scrapes. That's why I say that trophy bucks are easy to bag.

Taking The Dominant Buck During The Rut

When hunting a trophy buck during the rut, remember this trophy has greatly expanded his home range to locate more estrous does. So even though the buck may expose himself more often during daylight hours, being able to accurately predict where and when that buck will show up at a certain spot may become more difficult.

However, for the outdoorsman hunting property where he's not spotted a trophy buck all season, this may be good news. When the dominant buck expands his home range, he may cross property he hasn't frequented at any other time of the year, exposing himself to more hunters who are in search of a trophy buck. If I have one buck tag left to fill, and I'm hunting deer in the rut, I'll let little bucks pass by in hopes that I'll see a trophy buck that is expanding his territory.

Other hunters can also make bagging a trophy buck easier. Although most hunters say they want to take a trophy buck, the average hunter will generally harvest any buck, usually in that 1-1/2-year old age class, prior to the rut. To become a trophy hunter, the sportsman must be willing to let small bucks pass while he's waiting on a big buck. Few hunters are willing to do that, and competition for the trophy animals is much less.

Using A Magic Potion

All the world of deer hunting is searching for the magic potion that will lure a dominant buck to within gun range. One of the latest fads has been doe urine. Many sportsmen think that sprinkling the urine of a doe in estrus will draw a rutting buck to within gun range.

But there's a problem with this theory. The only way to tell if a doe is in estrus is to put her in a pen with a buck. If the buck mounts her, then she's in estrus. If the buck doesn't mount the doe, she's not. Trying to find the urine of a doe in estrus is a very complicated problem and can't be considered to be a magic elixir that always will lure in bucks, since does urinate every day. Knowing when a doe is in estrus is the key to collecting estrous urine and that's a wild guess at best.

A better buck attractant to use may be the urine of a dominant buck, which may have more effect on another dominant buck. Scientists have learned a difference does exist between the urine of a dominant buck and the other bucks in the herd. Only one dominant buck can live in a specific area. If the hunter can collect the urine of a dominant buck (probably the urine of a trophy deer that was killed somewhere else) and sprinkles some of that dominant buck urine in the scrape of the trophy buck he's trying to hunt, then this action may bring the trophy buck to that scrape quicker and more often. The trophy buck may feel he's being challenged by another dominant deer that has moved into his region.

Another tactic that should produce a dominant buck during the peak of the rut is to hunt the travel trails where you've seen nothing but does. If the hunter has found a region that does travel frequently during hunting season but has failed to see a buck in this area, the sportsman should return to this particular spot during the rut. Some time during the rut, one of those does will come into estrus. When she does, there will be a buck following

A dominant buck, like the one on the left, is often found with his harem of does during the rut.

her. If you're on your stand in the area where you've seen those does, then sooner or later those does will have a buck following them. Because he is the dominant buck, he claims the right to breed all the does in his dominance area, which makes him extremely vulnerable during the rut when his sex drive supersedes his natural wariness.

Hunting The Scrape Line

Trophy bucks have regular rounds they make- just like the policeman who walks a beat. During the rut, the buck will make scrapes all along this route. He may have some fresh scrapes, and there may be old scrapes too, which indicate that he's been using this particular itinerary for several weeks. By taking a stand along this route during the rut, the trophy may be easy to bag.

Another key that makes trophy buck hunting easy is that most often trophy deer will scrape in the same region year after year. When a dominant buck is harvested, the next deer in the pecking order that moves up to become the dominant buck will often scrape in the same places and

By using rattling antlers, you may be able to produce a trophy buck like this one.

meet his does at the same sites as the dominant buck before him did. That's why if you're hunting in a region with older age class deer, many times you can take several trophy bucks out of the same stand along the same scrape line several years in a row.

Using Rattling Antlers

Whenever anyone steps up and says that any tactic is a sure fire method to kill a trophy buck, you can recognize a lie. However, specific strategies under certain conditions sometimes will bring in a trophy buck- like using rattling.

There are two situations that make rattling work. When a dominant buck hears antlers clashing, he may assume other bucks are in his area fighting for dominance and that one of those bucks may want to challenge him. So he may come in to attempt to run off the competition.

Another probable reason rattling works is because of the deer's natural curiosity. I think a dominant buck will respond to rattling just to see which deer's going to get whipped in the fight. Rattling also will bring in does and subordinate bucks, therefore, rattling during the rut can be an effective tactic to kill a big buck. However, rattling also has the potential to cause a trophy buck not to come to you.

If the trophy buck is tending a doe that's in estrus, and he hears that rattling, he may not come because he doesn't want to run the risk of losing that doe in estrus to simply watch a fight or get involved in a fight. I've actually watched a dominant buck steer a doe away from an area where I was rattling.

Many authorities on antler rattling teach that the best time to try the rattling tactic for bucks is during the peak of the rut. However, I disagree. I've found the best time to take a trophy buck by rattling is just before the rut and just after the rut. Given the choice, a trophy buck will choose to do the loving instead of the fighting.

Rattling can be a productive technique for bagging a trophy buck before and after the rut. Perhaps the dominant one believes that two subordinate bucks have found a doe that has come into estrus early or late in the seasson, and are fighting over her when he hears horns slashing. He assumes that he can run the other bucks off and then he can breed the doe.

The Best Rattling Sequence

Bob Zaiglin waits 15 to 20 minutes to let the woods settle down before he begins to rattle.

You may have spooked the deer going into the area you want to rattle. Waiting until the woods are still for awhile before you go into your rattling sequence is the most productive method of hunting.

I begin by pounding the antlers into the ground and alternate the antler pounding. What I'm trying to imitate is the hoof action of bucks stomping the ground and the running of the deer. Often a buck is pursuing a doe, and the doe will keep running from him. I want to create a picture in the deer's mind that the first sound he hears is that of a buck chasing the doe and she is not willing to stand for the buck.

When two bucks are preparing for a sparring match, they pound the ground with their feet. I use the rattling antlers first to imitate the sound of pounding deer hooves. I'll give this pounding sound for 30 seconds to a minute. Many times I've brought deer in strictly to the pounding sound before I ever start rattling antlers together.

The next step is to clash the antlers together loudly. Something many hunters forget when they're using rattling antlers is that the deer have feet as well as antlers. Often I'll clash the antlers together, pound the ground, clash the antlers together again and twist them. I'll carry on this sequence for a minute to 1-1/2 minutes. Again the critical key is to pound the ground with antlers in between the rattling.

I know plenty of hunters have brought in bucks by just clashing antlers together, but when you're attempting to fool a wily whitetail, the smart hunter will do everything he can. Pounding the ground is just something extra that helps the deer paint a better picture of a fight in his mind and may be the little extra required to pull him into your gun sights. I believe that one of the reasons my tactics work so well on big bucks is that I make the antler rattling sound as realistic as possible.

Also I pay attention to what's happening around me. Many hunters will look down at the ground when they pound it, or they'll watch the antlers when they rattle them. But what I've learned is that if a big buck is coming in to antler rattling, he'll run in, take a quick look and when he doesn't see a fight, he'll run away just as rapidly. If the hunter is not ready to take the deer when the buck comes in, the sportsman may see that trophy buck but never get a shot. Therefore, during this period of clashing antlers and pounding the ground, look for the buck, and have your rifle at hand. This sequence should last only about one minute to 1-1/2-minutes.

To be able to simulate a deer fight with rattling antlers, you must understand what actually takes place when bucks battle. Two, 200-pound deer make a loud, clashing sound when they run together and hit. But then when they lock up, a pushing match results. The only time you'll hear the sound of antlers clashing again is when one buck stumbles and falls, and the other buck attempts to move in and take advantage of this opportunity. The buck that has fallen quickly will regain his feet. Then there will be another clash of antlers However, most of the sounds you'll hear in a buck fight will

Bob Zaiglin rattles up big bucks throughout the year.

be the grinding sounds of antlers. So when you're rattling, remember to grind more with the antlers and clash less.

After the 1-1/2 minutes of clashing, grinding and pounding the ground, I start looking around to see if I can spot a deer. I examine the terrain slowly, much like a turkey hunter, because the deer may be watching me. I've found that about 60 percent of the deer hunters rattle in are never seen.

After I've taken 30 seconds to 1-1/2 minutes to observe what's happening, I begin pounding the ground again with the antlers to simulate a deer stomping, and I start raking the brush with the antlers. Many hunters don't understand that rubbing a tree with the antlers is one of the most effective ways to bring in a buck. Many times I've brought in deer by only raking the antlers up and down the side of a tree, which can be done for as long or for as short time as the hunter feels he should. After you've raked the bushes and the brush, you've completed a sequence of rattling.

Rattling and Grunting Works In Any Area

Some of the early criticisms of rattling to bring in bucks included that these were trophy tactics that were successful in Texas and mainly worked there because the sex ratio was close to one buck for one doe. Critics also believed that rattling antlers only brought in trophy bucks. Many whitetail hunters would be satisfied to take a four or six point instead of waiting on a trophy buck.

I've rattled up more small deer than big deer, because yearling and two year old deer go crazy over rattling. That's why this technique will be the most productive in the North and South and other states where many mature bucks live. Remember very few places have a good number of trophy bucks. Young deer will come to rattling quicker because they are insecure and want to be around bigger and stronger bucks. These young bucks are like teenagers at a dance that want to be part of the social atmosphere and are eager to breed any chance they get. Therefore, these big buck tactics are even more effective on smaller, younger bucks.

CHAPTER 15

WEIRD WAYS TO BAG A BUCK

DEER ARE CURIOUS. This natural curiosity of the whitetail deer is one of the most overlooked aspects in most sportsmen's hunt plans.

A biologist friend of mine once told me about the war going on inside a deer's head much of the time. The deer's fear instinct causes him to flee from anything that is unnatural in the wild, anything he is unsure of or anything that startles him. But his natural curiosity often draws him back to the very thing from which he normally shies away.

Most often this phenomenon is more readily seen in younger deer, especially in younger bucks, rather than in older deer. An older buck doesn't obtain his age, his size and his antler development by continuously investigating unknown sights, sounds and smells. However, oftentimes the hunter can use the deer's natural curiosity to take young bucks and, on some occasions, even older bucks.

Chain Saws And Three-Wheelers

Some hunters I know in Tennessee had started using chain saws and three-wheelers to take deer. Many of these folks who loved to hunt also were pulp wooders. They began to take notice of deer coming in to areas where they were cutting timber. Often the deer would walk up within 10 or 15 yards of where they were cutting. Although they didn't understand why the deer came, they knew that for some reason, the sound of the chain saw seemed to attract the deer. So they decided to try and utilize chain saws to call deer.

These hunters took their chain saws into the woods during deer season, cranked them up and revved them on the edges of right-of-ways and woodsroads. Then after the hunters already had the saws running for a minute or two, they sat the chain saws on the ground and let them idle while they hid in the bushes. Sure enough, several of those guys bagged some nice deer hunting over chain saws.

Other hunters in the region who found out about the chain saw hunting started pulling their three-wheelers up to the edges of power line right-of-ways, woodsroads and/or firebreaks, revving up the engines and leaving them idling, because the noise of a three-wheeler was not that much different from the noise put out by a chain saw. Sure enough, the deer came in to the three-wheeler sounds too.

I asked a couple of wildlife biologists about the possibility of deer being lured by these sounds. They said they could understand how chain saw or three-wheeler noise might lure deer into a specific spot, particularly if pulp wooding already was taking place in the area. When the timber fell, acorns in the tops of the trees were brought to the ground where deer could feed on them. The chain saw noise lured deer because of their natural curiosity to investigate anything going on in their habitat, and it probably reminded them of a dinner bell ringing.

Luring Deer With Scents

For some unknown reason, the scent of a predator will lure deer in to a hunter. Fox urine is being used by some hunters to leave a scent trail that deer often will follow.

Some hunters are putting fox urine on scent pads on their feet and then walking through the woods to their treestands. They've also reported deer following the scent of the fox urine to their trees. The only explanation I can give is that because deer are curious, and the scent is so strong, the deer follow the smell to investigate it.

During an either-sex season, many hunters will scurry around and try to collect doe urine from does being butchered. However, the urine of big, dominant bucks may be a better prize. An effective tactic may be to collect the urine of a large, mature buck that has been taken, make a mock scrape and pour a little of that urine into the scrape.

When the dominant buck discovers that scrape and thinks another dominant buck is in his area scraping, he probably will become upset and start hanging around that scrape waiting for the intruding buck to appear into his territory. Because of the natural social order of deer, one buck in

In some areas, hunters use three-wheelers to call deer.

a given area establishes himself as the dominant buck. As the dominant buck, he claims the right to breed the does. Using the urine of another dominant buck in his territory may fool the first dominant buck into believing a second buck is contesting his right to breed the does. Also, adding more urine to the mock scrape each day may cause the dominant buck to check the scrape more regularly in hopes of finding the interloper and running him off.

The Front And Back Of Hunting Pressure

Many hunters realize if they can get in the woods before other sportsmen, the second group of outdoorsmen will spook the deer toward them, which is an effective way of taking deer. However, in areas where the hunting pressure is very intense, some outdoorsmen have learned how to hunt the front side and the back side of this hunting pressure.

Imagine a line of hunters all coming into the woods at the same time from the same direction. This mass stream of humanity will move all the deer in a region in front of them as they enter the woods. However, also realize that if these hunters are 50 to 100 yards apart when they come into the woods, the deer that have held tight and allowed the hunters to walk past them can slip out behind that wave of hunters. So there is a primary movement of deer away from hunters as the sportsmen come into the woods and a secondary movement of deer away from hunters after the sportsmen have passed by where the deer are hiding. To effectively use hunting pressure to bag deer, hunt both movement patterns.

Walking And Talking Like A Buck

When wildlife biologist Karl Miller was doing research on deer scrapes and rubs, he spent much time walking through the woods and hunting deer signs. As Miller walked, he carried a staff with him and tried to sound like a deer walking on four legs rather than a man walking on two. He used the staff to imitate as closely as he could the sounds he had heard deer make as they walked. While doing this, Miller had two or three different bucks come up to investigate and act as though they wanted to pick a fight.

One of Miller's friends bagged a nice deer with Miller using this technique. Miller was on one side of a hill trying to imitate a deer's walk when a big buck came running up from the other side of the hill to investigate the sounds he was making. When Miller saw the deer coming, he gave a tending grunt, the sound of a buck with a doe that encounters another buck. After Miller gave that sound, the buck came right on in, and Miller's friend took the deer. Making sounds like a deer walking and grunting caused that buck to come within gun range.

When you use this tactic, be sure to wear hunter orange since you're making the sounds for which other hunters are listening.

Bellying Up To Bucks

Most hunters are timid about doing something that may be considered a little weird, strange or unusual by other hunters.

Hunting pressure causes trophy bucks like this one to move.

Indians, who were some of the best deer hunters who ever lived, thought nothing weird or unusual about lying on their bellies on the forest floor and crawling to within bow range of a fat buck. Many of the Indians even dressed in a deer's skin to give the appearance of being a forest creature. However, when we think about lying down on the cold, dirty ground and crawling through the leaves where redbugs and ticks live, we reason only a person who has completely lost his mind will try such a tactic to bag a buck. But when you consider the money you spend to buy top-notch hunting equipment, all the time that is necessary to do an efficient

143

Sometimes you have to crawl to get a buck.

job of scouting and the hours involved in staying still in a treestand while looking and searching for a buck to harvest, then whatever antics you have to go through to bag a buck will seem justified.

A hunting companion of mine, Dr. Bob Sheppard, spotted a large six-point feeding down the edge of a field a few years ago. The deer was upwind of Sheppard who couldn't see a way to circle the deer and still be able to get a shot. Through the middle of the field was a small, 1-1/2-foot-wide drainage ditch with about 1-1/2 inches of water in it. The ditch offered the only access to intercept the deer's path without being detected.

Sheppard crawled into the ditch and through the water for about 100 yards until he reached a point above the deer where the wind was keeping Sheppard's scent away from the buck. Yet Sheppard still was in the buck's line of travel. Since the ditch was not large enough to sit up in, Sheppard rolled over on his back and looked at the sky. Occasionally he peered down toward his toes and saw the six-point still was coming in his direction.

When the deer was about 60 yards away from Sheppard, he knew if he looked again, the animal surely would spot him. He lay motionless in the ditch and listened for the deer. In about 15 minutes he heard the deer crunching acorns about 15 or 20 yards from where he was hiding. Sheppard rolled over on his left elbow and propped his rifle up. As the buck continued to feed with his head down, he was coming straight toward Sheppard.

When the crosshairs of Sheppard's scope settled between the deer's front shoulders, he squeezed the trigger - shooting through the deer's antlers and breaking the buck's spine. When Sheppard stepped off the distance from his spot in the ditch to where the animal lay motionless, the distance was only 10 paces. Although the buck only had six points, his antlers were massive, and he weighed over 200 pounds. Sheppard gladly would crawl 200 or 500 yards in the water on his belly to bag that buck again.

Crawling to a trophy may seem weird to some, but the folks I know who crawl on deer when necessary bag their bucks. The ones who are not willing to crawl, go home with tales of trophies that are too far away to take.

CONVENIENT ORDER FORM

I would like to have additional copies of this book

THE MASTERS' SECRETS OF DEER HUNTING

Please mail me _____ copies to the address below:

NAME _____

ADDRESS _____

CITY _____ STATE _____ ZIP _____

Number of books ordered _____ X $11.95 per book.

TOTAL AMOUNT ENCLOSED
(Check or Money Order) $_____

Postage and handling charges are included in the book price.

Please mail to:

Larsen's Outdoor Publishing
2640 Elizabeth Place
Lakeland, FL 33813

Please allow four weeks for delivery.

John E. Phillips' DEER HUNTING LIBRARY

<u>Masters' Secrets of Deer Hunting</u> is the first in a series of hunting books dedicated to the sportsmen who enjoy improving their techniques. The series, known as the Deer Hunting Library, includes complete details on the latest tactics and strategies for bagging deer, as well as expert tips from dozens of the nation's finest expert hunters.

These Editions Will Be Available Soon!

Deer Hunting - Truth And Fiction
The Science of Deer Hunting
and others...

Also Watch for the
TURKEY HUNTING LIBRARY
Coming Soon!

Don't Miss Them!

If you want to receive our catalog and other information about the availability of additional books in John E. Phillips' Hunting Library, please fill out the following and mail today!

Yes, keep me updated on the Hunting Library books!

Name_____

Address_____

City_____State _____Zip_____

Mail to:
Larsen's Outdoor Publishing, Dept. DB1
2640 Elizabeth Place
Lakeland, FL 33813

OLD EIGHT BALL

Image Size 15" x 23"

ABOUT THE ARTIST

At age 25, Eddie LeRoy of Eufaula, Alabama, is considered one of the most talented and potentially great wildlife artists in the country. He has won the Alabama Wildlife Federation's 1989-90 Art Competition, the 1990-91 Florida Wild Turkey Stamp Competition and placed in the top nine in the National Wild Turkey Federation Competition. LeRoy was chosen by Waterfowl U.S.A. to be the 1990-91 sponsored Print Artist of the Year. Besides being an artist, LeRoy is an ardent angler and proficient hunter.

LeRoy's original paintings and prints steadily have grown in value each year. LeRoy's art is a wise investment for the outdoor sportsman. His work has appeared in <u>Deer and Deer Hunting</u>, <u>Hunter's World</u>, <u>Buckmasters</u>, <u>Alabama Conservation</u>, <u>Alabama Wildlife</u>, <u>Turkey Call</u>, <u>B.A.S.S. Masters</u> and <u>Southern Outdoors</u> magazines and Aqua-Field Publications.

Printed on acid-free paper. The cost is $45 per print, plus $5 for shipping and handling for a total of $50. Send check or money order to:

Night Hawk Publications
P.O. Drawer 375
Fairfield, Al 35064
Ph: (205) 786-3630;786-4022

Please allow four weeks for delivery.

FOR THE HUNTERS
WHO ALSO FISH!

LARRY LARSEN'S BASS SERIES LIBRARY!

**1. FOLLOW THE FORAGE FOR BETTER BASS ANGLING -
VOLUME 1 BASS/PREY RELATIONSHIP** - The most important key to catching bass is finding them in a feeding mood. Knowing the predominant forage, its activity and availability, as well as its location in a body of water will enable an angler to catch more and larger bass. Whether you fish artificial lures or live bait, you will benefit from this book.
SPECIAL FEATURES
> o PREDATOR/FORAGE INTERACTION
> o BASS FEEDING BEHAVIOR
> o UNDERSTANDING BASS FORAGE
> o FORAGE ACTIVITY CHART

**2. FOLLOW THE FORAGE FOR BETTER BASS ANGLING -
VOLUME 2 TECHNIQUES** - Beginners and veterans alike will achieve more success utilizing proven concepts that are based on predator/forage interactions. Understanding the reasons behind lure or bait success will result in highly productive, bass-catching patterns.
SPECIAL FEATURES
> o LURE SELECTION CRITERIA
> o EFFECTIVE PATTERN DEVELOPMENT
> o NEW BASS CATCHING TACTICS
> o BAIT AND LURE METHODS

3. BASS PRO STRATEGIES - Professional fishermen have opportunities to devote extended amounts of time to analyzing a body of water and planning a productive day on it. They know how changes in pH, water temperature, color and fluctuations affect bass fishing, and they know how to adapt to weather and topographical variations. This book reveals the methods that the country's most successful tournament anglers have employed to catch bass almost every time out.
SPECIAL FEATURES
> o MAPPING & WATER ELIMINATION
> o LOCATE DEEP & SHALLOW BASS
> o BOAT POSITION FACTORS
> o WATER CHEMISTRY INFLUENCES

4. BASS LURES - TRICKS & TECHNIQUES - Modifications of lures and development of new baits and techniques continue to keep the fare fresh, and that's important. Bass seem to become "accustomed" to the same artificials and presentations seen over and over again. As a result, they become harder to catch. It's the new approach that again sparks the interest of some largemouth. To that end, this book explores some of the latest ideas for modifying, rigging and using them anywhere in the country.
SPECIAL FEATURES
> o UNIQUE LURE MODIFICATIONS
> o IN-DEPTH VARIABLE REASONING
> o PRODUCTIVE PRESENTATIONS
> o EFFECTIVE NEW RIGGINGS

5. SHALLOW WATER BASS - Catching shallow water largemouth is not particularly difficult. Catching lots of them usually is. Even more challenging is catching lunker-size bass in seasons other than during the spring spawn. Anglers applying the information within the covers of this book on marshes, estuaries, reservoirs, lakes, creeks or small ponds should triple their results. The book details productive new tactics to apply to thin-water angling. Numerous photographs and figures easily define the optimal locations and proven methods to catch bass.
SPECIAL FEATURES
> o LOCATING BASS CONCENTRATIONS
> o ANALYSIS OF WATER TYPES
> o TACTICS FOR SPECIFIC HABITATS
> o LARSEN'S "FLORA FACTOR"

6. BASS FISHING FACTS - This angler's guide to the lifestyles and behavior of the black bass is a reference source of sorts, never before compiled. The book explores the behavior of bass during pre- and post-spawn as well as during bedding season. It examines how bass utilize their senses to feed and how they respond to environmental factors. The book details how fishermen can be more productive by applying such knowledge to their bass angling. The information within the covers of this book includes those bass species, known as "other" bass, such as redeye, Suwannee, spotted, etc.
SPECIAL FEATURES
> o BASS FORAGING MOTIVATORS
> o DETAILED SPRING MOVEMENTS
> o A LOOK AT BASS SENSES
> o GENETIC INTRODUCTION/STUDIES

7. TROPHY BASS - is focused at today's dedicated lunker hunters who find more enjoyment in wrestling with one or two monster largemouth than with a "panfull" of yearlings. To help the reader better understand how to catch big bass, a majority of this book explores productive techniques for trophies. The "how to" information was gleaned from professional guides and other experienced trophy bass hunters. This book takes a look at geographical areas and waters that offer opportunities to catch giant bass.

SPECIAL FEATURES

- o GEOGRAPHIC DISTRIBUTIONS
- o STATE RECORD INFORMATION
- o GENETIC GIANTS
- o TECHNIQUES FOR TROPHIES

8. AN ANGLER'S GUIDE TO BASS PATTERNS examines the most effective combination of lure, method and places. Being able to develop a pattern of successful methods and lures for specific habitats and environmental conditions is the key to catching several bass on each fishing trip. Understanding bass movements and activities and the most appropriate and effective techniques to employ will add many pounds of enjoyment to the sport of bass fishing. "Bass Patterns" is a reference source for all anglers, regardless of where they live or their skill level.

SPECIAL FEATURES

- o BOAT POSITIONING
- o NEW WATER STRATEGIES
- o DEPTH AND COVER CONCEPTS
- o MOVING WATER TACTICS
- o WEATHER/ACTIVITY FACTORS

9. BASS GUIDE TIPS focuses on the most productive methods of the top bass fishing guides in the country. This book is loaded with sometimes regionally-known techniques that will work in waters all around the country. Often such "local knowledge" remains regional or lake-specific, but this book explains how one productive tactic on a southern lake might be just as productive on waters in the midwest or north.

SPECIAL FEATURES

- o SHINERS, SUNFISH KITES & FLIES
- o FLIPPIN', PITCHIN' & DEAD STICKIN'
- o BRACKISH WATERS & BASS SIGNS
- o FRONTS, HIGH WINDS & RAIN
- o MOVING, DEEP, HOT & COLD WATERS

Frank Sargeant's INSHORE LIBRARY!

_____ THE SNOOK BOOK

"Must" reading for anyone who loves the pursuit of this unique sub-tropic species. Every aspect of finding and catching big snook is covered, in every season and in all waters where snook are found.

_____ THE REDFISH BOOK

Packed with expertise from the nation's leading redfish anglers and guides, this book covers every aspect of finding and fooling giant reds. Dozens of secret techniques are revealed for the first time

LARSEN'S OUTDOOR PUBLISHING
CONVENIENT ORDER FORM
ALL PRICES INCLUDE POSTAGE/HANDLING

FRESH WATER
___BSL1. Better Bass Angling Vol 1 ($13.95)
___BSL2. Better Bass Angling Vol 2 ($13.95)
___BSL3. Bass Pro Strategies ($13.95)
___BSL4. Bass Lures/Techniques ($13.95)
___BSL5. Shallow Water Bass ($13.95)
___BSL6. Bass Fishing Facts ($13.95)
___BSL7. Trophy Bass ($13.95)
___BSL8. Bass Patterns ($13.95)
___BSL9. Bass Guide Tips ($13.95)
___CF1. Mstrs' Scrts/Crappie Fshng ($12.45)
___CF2. Crappie Tactics ($12.45)
___CF3. Mstr's Secrets of Catfishing ($12.45)
___LB1. Larsen on Bass Tactics ($15.95)
___PF1. Peacock Bass Explosions! ($16.95)
___PF2. Peacock Bass & Other Fierce
     Exotics ($17.95)

SALT WATER
___IL1. The Snook Book ($13.95)
___IL2. The Redfish Book ($13.95)
___IL3. The Tarpon Book ($13.95)
___IL4. The Trout Book ($13.95)
___SW1. The Reef Fishing Book ($16.45)

OTHER OUTDOORS BOOKS
___DL1. Diving to Adventure ($12.45)
___DL2. Manatees/Vanishing ($12.45)
___DL3. Sea Turtles/Watchers' ($12.45)
___OC1. Outdoor Chuckle Book ($9.95)

REGIONAL
___FG1. Secret Spots-Tampa Bay/
     Cedar Key ($15.95)
___FG2. Secret Spots - SW Florida ($15.95)
___BW1. Guide/North Fl. Waters ($14.95)
___BW2. Guide/Cntral Fl.Waters ($14.95)
___BW3. Guide/South Fl.Waters ($14.95)
___OT1. Fish/Dive - Caribbean ($11.95)
___OT3. Fish/Dive Florida/ Keys ($13.95)

HUNTING
___DH1. Mstrs' Secrets/ Deer Hunting ($13.95)
___DH2. Science of Deer Hunting ($13.95)
___DH3. Mstrs' Secrets/Bowhunting ($12.45)
___DH4. How to Take Monster Bucks ($13.95)
___TH1. Mstrs' Secrets/ Turkey Hunting ($13.95)
___OA1. Hunting Dangerous Game! ($9.95)
___OA2. Game Birds & Gun Dogs ($9.95)
___BP1. Blackpowder Hunting Secrets ($14.45)

VIDEO &
SPECIAL DISCOUNT PACKAGES
___ V1 - Video - Advanced Bass Tactics $29.95
___BSL - Bass Series Library (9 vol. set) $94.45
___ IL - Inshore Library (4 vol. set) $42.95
___ BW - Guides to Bass Waters (3 vols.) $37.95
Volume sets are autographed by each author.

> **BIG MULTI-BOOK DISCOUNT!**
> **2-3 books, SAVE 10%**
> **4 or more books, SAVE 20%**

> **INTERNATIONAL ORDERS**
> **Send check in U.S. funds; add $6**
> **more per book for airmail rate**

ALL PRICES INCLUDE POSTAGE/HANDLING

No. of books _____ x $_____ ea =$_____   *Special Package* _____ @ $_____
No. of books _____ x $_____ ea =$_____   *Video (50-min) $29.95 =* $_____
   Multi-book Discount (%) $_____   *(Pkgs include discount)= N/A*
    SUBTOTAL 1 $_____   *SUBTOTAL 2* $_____

> _____**For Priority Mail (add $2 more per book)** $_____
> **TOTAL ENCLOSED (check or money order)** $_____

NAME_____ADDRESS_____

CITY_____STATE_____ZIP_____

Send check or Money Order to: Larsen's Outdoor Publishing, Dept. 97-BK
2640 Elizabeth Place, Lakeland, FL 33813 (941)644-3381
(Sorry, no credit card orders)

NIGHT HAWK PUBLICATIONS

Please send me the following books:

_____ **DEER & FIXINGS COOKBOOK**
by John & Denise Phillips
More than 50 years combined experience in preparing
venison, a heart-smart meat with fewer calories and less
fat and cholesterol but more protein than chicken,
contains information on field and home care of venison
as well as more than 100 proven venison recipes and more
than 100 recipes for side dishes to accompany venison.
$14 each, which includes postage and handling.

_____ **OUTDOOR LIFE'S COMPLETE TURKEY
HUNTING**   by John Phillips
Includes the newest tactics from more than 35 of the best
turkey hunters across the nation for hunting gobblers as
well as more than 180 drawings and photos.
$27.95 each, which includes postage and handling.

_____ **FISH & FIXINGS COOKBOOK**
by John & Denise Phillips
For all heart and health-conscious outdoorsmen, more
than 125 delicious recipes for grilling, broiling, baking
and frying saltwater and freshwater fish. More than 125
recipes for side dishes and numerous tips on handling
fresh and frozen fish.
$14 each, which includes postage and handling.

Name_____

Address_____

City_____State_____Zip_____

Send check or money order to:

**Night Hawk Publications
P.O. Drawer 375
Fairfield, Al 35064
Ph: (205) 786-3630;786-4022**

Please allow four weeks for delivery.